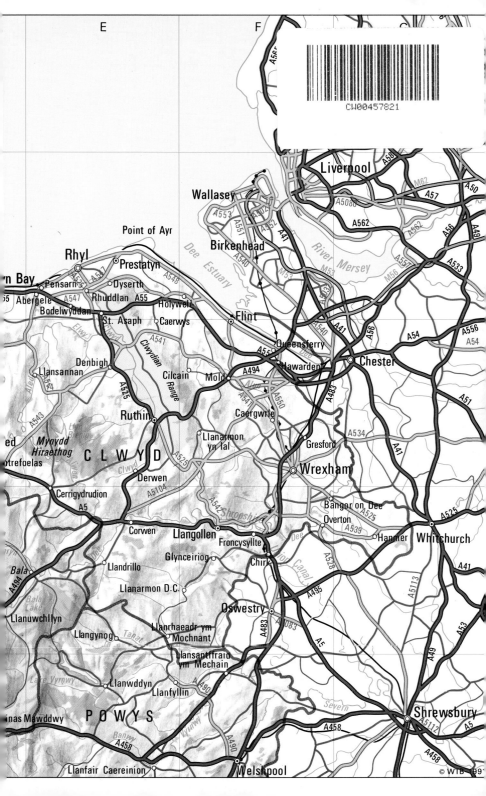

WHERE TO GO – AT A GLANCE

For quick, easy reference, here is a list of all the attractions and places to visit featured in this book together with the pages on which you'll find the relevant information.

Conwy Castle

Bodnant Garden

Ffestiniog Railway

Cabin Lift, Llandudno

NORTH WALES GAZETTEER

The A–Z gazetteer of resorts, cities, towns and villages starts here. It's all laid out in an informative, easy-to-follow style. Each entry contains a description of the destination in question followed by a list of its attractions and places to visit. These range from castles to slate caverns, wildlife parks to woollen mills, adventure parks to narrow-gauge railways. There are also quite a few highly individualistic places open to visitors, such as the unique fantasy village of Portmeirion, and the mountain at Llanberis which has been hollowed out as part of a mammoth scheme to provide hydro-electricity.

Attractions and places to visit are high-lighted in **bold italic** at the end of each entry. It is impossible, in a guide of this nature, to give precise opening details for each attraction. The vast majority will be open at all reasonable hours from April to the end of September.

Many will also stay open (often on a limited basis) in the winter months. Telephone numbers are provided, so you can check for yourself – or call into a Tourist Information Centre for details of local places to visit.

KEY TO SYMBOLS

_i_ Tourist Information Centre

A5 Each entry has a map reference to enable you to locate it on the gridded North Wales map on pages 2/3

C/F (following telephone number): Admission is charged/free. Please note that for some entries – such as castles which can

be viewed from exterior only and cathedrals – it is not appropriate to include C/F information

⊕ **Cadw: Welsh Historic Monuments site**

National Trust site

National Museum of Wales site

ABERDARON
GWYNEDD   A5

A strong sense of Welshness surrounds the coastal community of Aberdaron on the remote western tip of the Llŷn peninsula. Welsh is very much the predominant language in these parts, nurtured by Aberdaron's off-the-beaten-track location 'at the end of the earth'. The village of stone and lime-washed dwellings crowds into a shallow valley beside a long, sandy beach. There's a Celtic, almost Irish, feel to the place, which is surrounded by a haphazard patchwork of fields studded with white-painted farmsteads.

But Aberdaron's self-contained personality, untroubled by the world outside, is to some extent misleading. It is a popular holiday village in summer; in times gone by, it was also a busy spot when pilgrims gathered here before the final leg of their journey to Bardsey island, 2 miles offshore. Three pilgrimages to Bardsey, on which a monastic community was founded in AD615, equalled one to Rome. A 14th-century building in Aberdaron – now a café and gift shop – was once a house where pilgrims rested before crossing the treacherous waters of Bardsey Sound to the 'Isle of 20,000 Saints'.

Aberdaron stands amongst Llŷn's wildest seashores

Aberdaron was the birthplace of Richard Roberts Jones (1780–1843), better known as Dic Aberdaron. This strange character taught himself no less than

35 languages and compiled a dictionary in Welsh, Hebrew and Greek.

The village is tucked away behind a headland that shelters it from the westerly winds, which can blow forcefully in these parts. For a breathtaking view of Llŷn's savagely beautiful coastline and Bardsey island follow the road west from Aberdaron for 2 miles or so to the 160m (524ft) summit of Mynydd Mawr and the cliffs of Braich-y-Pwll, the 'Land's End of North Wales'. The land ends very abruptly indeed, plunging down to the sea in a curtain of jagged cliffs.

From the summit, Bardsey – whose name is of Norse origin – presents an intimidating sight. The bulky island, rising to 167m (548ft) above the swirling, dangerous waters, is known in Welsh as Ynys Enlli, the 'Isle of the currents' or 'Tide-race island'. The poor pilgrims would pray for safe passage at St Mary's Church, whose ruins can still be traced amongst the headland's bracken-covered slopes. St Mary's Well, an unusual holy well associated with the church, still survives at the foot of the cliffs below. This freshwater spring, which was thought to have miraculous healing powers, becomes completely covered by the sea at high tide. Following in the footsteps of the pilgrims is nowadays difficult, for there is no regular access to Bardsey, which is privately owned by an environmental trust.

Porth-oer, 2½ miles north of Aberdaron in a rare break in the cliffs, is also known as Whistling Sands. The grains of sand on this attractive crescent-shaped beach are supposed to whistle or squeak underfoot.

ABERFFRAW

GWYNEDD   B3

Aberffraw, tucked away on the Isle of Anglesey's western shores, stands above a narrow, sandy inlet and a large, open area of grassy dunes. It is difficult to believe that the village was once the 'capital' of North Wales, home of the princes of Gwynedd – including Llywelyn the Great – who held court here from the 9th to the 13th centuries. Aberffraw's royal palace has long since disappeared, though a Norman arch reset in St Beuno's Church may be a sole survivor from the building. Llywelyn, 'Prince of Aberffraw and Lord of Snowdonia', is remembered in the name of the Llys Llywelyn Coastal Heritage Centre, which is located in a collection of beautifully renovated stone buildings.

The coastline around and about is mostly low-lying and sandy. There's an excellent beach along Aberffraw Bay just south of the village. Porth Cwyfan west of Aberffraw is another delightful spot. On the shores of this rocky cove is a little island (normally accessible by foot) with a tiny 12th-century church.

Nearby are the vast Malltraeth sands which flank the wooded estuary of the river Cefni. The estuary and canalized Malltraeth marsh inland are good birdwatching areas, especially for winter wildfowl. This part of Anglesey inspired the work of the

famous wildlife artist Charles Tunnicliffe, who spent the last 30 years of his life at Malltraeth. There is an exhibition of his work at Llangefni (see entry).

The Church of St Cadwaladr in the nearby village of Llangadwaladr has associations with the Welsh princes. Its finest treasure is a stained glass window depicting the saint. The small lake of Llyn Coron lies to the north.

Llys Llywelyn Coastal Heritage Centre. Tel (0407) 840845/6. F. Anglesey's rich wildlife and heritage explained in displays and audio-visual theatre. Guided walks.

Nearby
Glantraeth Children's Animal Park, Bodorgan (on minor road off B4422). Tel (0407) 840897. C. Birds, animals, pony rides, adventure playground.

ABERGELE

CLWYD   E2

Abergele is a town which has Pensarn (see separate entry) as its seaside arm. Although Abergele is best known as a seaside town, limestone outcrops to the south introduce visitors to a rural area reaching across the Denbigh moors, a stretch of upland known as Mynydd Hiraethog. The nearest English approximation to hiraethog is 'place of longing', a reflection of the rich seam of history and heritage that underlies Hiraethog's now-empty moorlands. Far removed from the frenetic activity of the busy coast, this is an area which rewards leisurely exploration of its peaceful villages, lakes, rivers and forests.

The town's strong country connections are proved on Monday mornings with the arrival of gumbooted farmers driving their vehicles and trailers to the weekly livestock market. At weekends a general market in the town centre adds to the image of a centre offering a flavour of both the seaside and the country as its *raison d'étre*.

Market day at Abergele

ABERSOCH
GWYNEDD   B4

Abersoch is a popular sailing centre

Two sandy beaches and a pretty harbour have made Abersoch a popular resort, especially with the yachting community. The little village, built on a hill around the river Soch on the south-western tip of the Llŷn peninsula, has developed to reflect its obvious tourist appeal. Hotels, cafés and gift shops line the main streets and facilities on offer include boat trips to Ynys Enlli (Bardsey island), pony trekking and golf.

At the more tranquil Llanengan, 1½ miles west, St Engan's Church boasts two naves, two altars and two carved rood screens. An inscription on one of the roofbeams notes that the church was restored in 1847 by D Williams, a Caernarfon builder, but most of the structure dates back to 1534 or earlier, for the original church was founded by St Engan in the 6th century. Engan, or einion, is the Welsh for anvil, and the church banner depicts an anvil alongside a Celtic cross and daffodil.

From the churchyard visitors can enjoy still, unspoilt views across to Llŷn's mountainous spine. About 90m (100 yards) away is Ffynnon Engan (Engan's Well).

AMLWCH
GWYNEDD   B2

In the old days, Amlwch was one of the Isle of Anglesey's busiest ports. Its past role is explained by a strange area on the southern approach to the town. This is Parys mountain, a lunar-like wasteland burnished in hues of red, magenta and yellow and pock-marked with craters and abandoned workings.

In the 18th century, this was the world's most productive copper mine. As production grew, so did Amlwch. It must have been a raucous frontier town, for records state that its 6000 inhabitants were served by no less than 1025 ale houses. The copper ore was shipped out from the narrow, rock-bound inlet of Amlwch Port – how did those fleets of ore-carriers ever fit into such a small place? – which today is a picturesque harbour filled with fishing and holiday craft.

Safe anchorage at Amlwch's narrow, sheltered harbour

The Parys Mines Company was responsible for building Amlwch's handsome parish church in 1800. The town's Roman Catholic church is also noteworthy, though not for aesthetic reasons: built to an uncompromisingly modern design, it resembles the upturned hull of a boat.

Point Lynas and the beach of Porth Eilian east of Amlwch stand below Mynydd Eilian, an exposed mountainside of scattered settlements. A lighthouse at the point warns shipping of Anglesey's rocky north coast. Bull Bay takes a giant-sized bite out of the rugged shore 1 1/2 miles north-west of Amlwch. On the slopes above the bay's pretty little harbour there is an 18-hole golf course.

BALA/BALA LAKE

GWYNEDD   E4

Mountain-backed Bala Lake

Bala stands at the eastern end of 4-mile-long Llyn Tegid (Bala Lake), the largest natural lake in Wales. The town, which basically consists of one long, tree-lined main street of shops, inns and eating places, is traditionally Welsh in tone and temperament. The scene is set by a statue of the Liberal MP and advocate of home rule for Wales, Thomas Edward Ellis (1859–99), in suitably flamboyant pose.

Bala's strong associations with Wales's cultural and religious traditions include its links with the Rev Thomas Charles (1755–1814). There is a memorial plaque above the former home (now Barclays Bank) of this inspirational leader of Welsh Nonconformism and the Sunday School movement, who preached to packed congregations wherever he went. Another plaque is dedicated to Mary Jones, a 16-year-old who walked 28 miles to Bala from Cader Idris, barefoot part of the way, to ask Charles for a Bible.

The town has grown up around an earthwork, Tomen y Bala, possibly of Norman or even Iron Age origin. Its wooded mound, surrounded by houses, now looks comically out of place. Bala is a magnificent touring centre for Snowdonia and Mid Wales.

Its lake occupies a natural fault between the Aran and Arennig mountains. Fishing and watersports are excellent, though anglers will be lucky to catch the elusive gwyniad, a white fish of the salmon species which hides in its deep waters and is reputedly unique to the lake.

The Bala Adventure and Watersports Centre, between the lake and the banks of the river Tryweryn, offers facilities, courses and activities; the National White Water Centre has a full programme of canoeing events on the river Tryweryn

A one-hour trip along the shore of Bala Lake can be made on a narrow-gauge railway, which travels between Bala and Llanuwchllyn (see Llanuwchllyn entry).

Spectacular mountain roads lead south and north from Bala through lonely upland wildernesses (take the road to mountain-locked Lake Vyrnwy, for example, and complete the circular tour by returning along Bwlch y Groes, the highest road in Wales).

Bala Lake Railway. Tel (06784) 666. C. Lakeside narrow-gauge line. One of the 'Great Little Trains of Wales'. Main terminus at nearby Llanuwchllyn (see entry).

BANGOR

GWYNEDD   C3

Bangor is the northern centre for the University of Wales, and its 'College on the Hill' watches over the town like a latter-day fortress. Several major facilities are connected with the university: Theatr Gwynedd, housed in a modern square block, which is the venue for English and Welsh drama; the Ffriddoedd Road Sports Centre; and the Treborth Botanical Gardens, where you can wander through

Bangor's delightful Victorian pier

9 hectares (22 acres) of gardens and moorland. The long, low university building, with its regimented ranks of windows, is a 19th-century echo of the earlier focus for the city, Bangor Cathedral.

St Deiniol founded the original church in the 6th century, 70 years before Canterbury was established; but the present sombre version is a restored 13th- to 15th-century building. One of its greatest treasures is a 1518 carving given to the cathedral by Lord Mostyn which shows Christ bound and seated on a rock. The simple, life-sized figure makes a moving contrast to the detailed Victorian stained-glass windows behind it. A Bible Garden next to the cathedral was devised in 1962 and consists only of plants mentioned in the scriptures.

Across the road and towards the shopping centre is the Museum of Welsh Antiquities, which, along with an art gallery showing changing exhibitions, is housed in the Old Canonry. Here, Welsh life is covered from prehistory to the 19th century, using local finds, antiques and paintings.

From the busy High Street it's possible to get an idea of Bangor's layout. Between shop roofs, there are views of the university college, facing the city from the ridge of a rocky valley. The city centre, strung along the opposite slope, has several new shopping malls and a market on Fridays and Saturdays at James Street car park.

Bangor sits right on the edge of the Menai Strait: the woods of Anglesey seem almost within touching distance, especially from the end of the charming pier, now restored to its Victorian elegance. Ferries make daily sailings along the Strait from here in good weather during the holiday season.

Penrhyn Castle, an immense, neo-Norman stately home, overlooks the North Wales coast about 1½ miles from Bangor. Towers, turrets and arches recall a style which predated even Edward I's medieval fortresses, but the castle actually took on its present form in the 19th century, when the estate was owned by the Pennants, who earned great wealth from the nearby slate quarries. Thomas Hopper was the architect who designed the castle and its sumptuous interior, which is preserved in detail, right down to copies of the *Slate Trade Gazette* scattered on exquisitely carved tables. A tour by personal stereo takes visitors through lavish state rooms, where luxuries include original Chinese hand-painted wallpaper and a solid slate bed. A doll museum, which includes 300-year-old toys, is housed in what was once the master bedroom.

Bangor Cathedral. Founded in the 6th century. Present building restored in 19th century.

Museum of Welsh Antiquities and Art Gallery, Old Canonry, Ffordd Gwynedd. Tel (0248) 353368. F. Display of everyday items illustrates past life in rural Wales.

Theatr Gwynedd, Deiniol Road. Tel (0248) 351708. Varied programme, with popular entertainment in summer season.

Nearby
Cochwillan Old Hall, Tal-y-bont. Tel (0248) 364608. C. Well-preserved 15th-century hall with fine timber roof. Visitors are shown around by people who live in adjoining house. Must telephone for appointment.

Cochwillan Watermill, Tal-y-bont. Tel (0248) 362800. C. Working mill where you can see spinning wheels and jennys, looms and other traditional industrial machinery.

Penrhyn Castle (1 mile east of Bangor). Tel (0248) 353084. C. Fabulous 19th-century 'sham', magnificent inside and out. 🦋

Immaculate Penrhyn Castle was built with the wealth generated by North Wales's slate industry

CRAFTS

Call in at a craft workshop

Ruthin's superb Craft Centre

A novice potter at work

North Wales is home to a thriving crafts scene. The region's craggy mountains, hidden valleys and endless seascapes inspire craftspeople in many ways.

Potters and woodcarvers, ceramics and textile artists welcome visitors into their workshops. Some craftsworkers are based at modern, purpose-built centres, others have more isolated workshops in old farm buildings deep in the countryside. Much of the pleasure in visiting North Wales's crafts workshops comes from their idyllic surroundings. The Cwm Pottery, for example, is situated at Trefor on the slopes of the brooding Yr Eifl mountain range on the Llŷn peninsula. Crafts can also be most entertaining. At the Piggery Pottery in Llanberis you can try your hand at throwing your own pot, or paint your own designs on a pre-thrown item.

The tradition of woollen weaving in Wales goes back nearly 2000 years. At Trefriw Woollen Mills, visitors can tour the premises and view the processes of carding, spinning, dyeing and weaving. The friendly Bodeilio Craft Centre on the Isle of Anglesey allows its visitors to watch high-quality knitwear being manufactured (other facilities here include a mill shop, craft shop and tea room). Clover Casuals near Flint, manufacturers of unique hand-appliquéd and embroidered knitwear, also welcome visitors to their workshops, which are housed in an old schoolhouse.

If you want to see a number of craftspeople working together, then visit Ruthin where the Craft Centre has 13 individual studios arranged around a landscaped courtyard, together with a high-quality gallery, shop and restaurant. An old malthouse in Llangollen has recently been converted into a craft centre, and the Padarn Country Park at Llanberis contains a number of small craft workshops, one of which is occupied by a harp maker.

Another way of seeing a number of crafts all at once is to pop along to one of the many craft or medieval fairs held throughout North Wales. Crafts are also a feature of annual summer events such as the Llangollen International Musical Eisteddfod, the Conwy Festival and the Anglesey Show – look out here for the north's more unusual crafts skills, which include the making of rocking horses, stained glass and authentic costume dolls.

Traditional Welsh weaves

Water and stone defences at Beaumaris Castle

BEAUMARIS

GWYNEDD   C2

This Anglesey resort and sailing centre, on the eastern approaches to the Menai Strait, is more reminiscent of a genteel English watering place than a Welsh seaside town. Spacious stretches of seafront lawns, fine Georgian architecture, and streets of gabled Victorian and Edwardian villas give Beaumaris an identity which is anything but traditionally Welsh.

The architecture is an accurate reflection of the town's history. From early times, Beaumaris was a garrison town and seat of English influence. The town's name has distinctly foreign roots. It is based on the French *beau marais* meaning 'fair marsh', a reference to the site chosen by the 13th-century English king Edward I for a stronghold built to control the Welsh.

Beaumaris Castle was the final, and some say the finest, of Edward's 'iron ring' of North Wales fortresses. It might lack the grandeur of Caernarfon or the gritty presence of Conwy, but in pure architectural terms Beaumaris is undoubtedly the most sophisticated. The castle's lack of immediate visual impact is due to the fact that it was never finished. It was begun in 1295, but by 1298 the money had run out, leaving Beaumaris's defences with a stunted, incomplete look.

It is a different story from the air. A bird's-eye view brings into perspective the castle's beautifully symmetrical – and deadly effective – concentric 'rings within rings' system of defences. Like most of Edward's castles, Beaumaris was accessible from the sea. The tidal channel that linked it with the Menai Strait has long since disappeared, though the castle's dock, beside its fortified 'Gate next the Sea', is still filled with water. Along with North Wales's other great medieval castles, Beaumaris is a World Heritage Listed Site.

The town of Beaumaris is fortunate enough to have almost an embarrassment of historic riches. The Tudor Rose along Castle Street is a small black-and-white half-timbered house, built in about 1400 and one of the oldest surviving dwellings in Wales. Ye Olde Bull's Head nearby is another genuine antique. It was already centuries old when both Dr Johnson and Charles Dickens stayed there.

The building opposite the castle bearing the date 1614 is the Beaumaris Courthouse. Unusually, the wooden seating is arranged in such a way that the jury sits higher than the judge. Although the stone-flagged floors and hammerbeam roof have been retained, it is no museum piece, for the courthouse is one of the oldest still operating in Britain (it is also open to the public).

Beaumaris's chilling Victorian gaol is thankfully no longer in use. This stark stone building, restored and open to visitors, is just as it was in the 19th century. Its dank cells, workrooms, condemned cell, soundproofed punishment room and exercise yard complete with treadmill present a forbidding picture.

If this exposure to crime and punishment is too much for you, then visit the Museum of Childhood, a magical collection of toys, dolls, games, paintings and pottery spanning 150 years. The Time Tunnel along the seafront is another entertaining attraction, which tells of the history of this part of North Wales in an imaginative 'light and sound experience'.

The Church of St Mary and St Nicholas, with its battlemented roofline and robust square tower, is perfectly in tune with Beaumaris the castle stronghold and garrison town. Dating from the 14th century, it contains the stone coffin of Joan, daughter of King John and wife of the Welsh leader Llywelyn the Great.

For one of the finest views in North Wales, walk along the splendid Victoria Terrace to the pier and gaze across the Menai Strait to the mountains of Snowdonia. The view back towards the town is also most pleasing, recalling the prosperous, fashionable Beaumaris of the 19th century.

The town hosts a well-regarded and wide-ranging annual festival in early summer.

Beaumaris Castle. Tel (0248) 810361. C. Perfectly planned medieval fortress, the last – and largest – castle in North Wales built by Edward I. ✪

Beaumaris Courthouse. Tel (0248) 810367. C. Unique survival of an old courtroom.

Beaumaris Gaol. Tel (0248) 810921 or 750262 ext. 269. C. Grim reminder of the harshness of prison life in Victorian times.

Museum of Childhood. Tel (0248) 810448. C. A nostalgic collection. Enchants young and old alike.

Time Tunnel. Tel (0248) 810072. C. Audio-visual experience. Also tells the story of emigration to America.

BEDDGELERT ℹ️
GWYNEDD   C4

When you arrive at Beddgelert, you'll find it difficult to understand why the locals took the trouble to invent the story of the faithful hound Gelert in order to attract visitors. Beddgelert enjoys such an outstanding location that its natural beauty is enough in itself to guarantee a visit from anyone touring Snowdonia.

But first, let's dispense with the legend. Follow the path beside the rushing river Glaslyn to a stone monument in the fields south of the village. This supposedly marks the resting place of Gelert, the dog left by Prince Llywelyn to guard his child. The poor dog, covered in blood, was killed by his master before he realized that the heroic hound had, in fact, saved his child from a wolf. The story, which has been attributed to the fertile imagination of an

18th-century innkeeper, has a certain enduring quality, probably explained by Britain's reputation as a nation of dog-lovers.

The village of dark-stoned houses stands in a splendid spot amongst massive rock buttresses, steep mountain slopes and wooded hillsides at the south-western gateway to the central peaks of Snowdonia. Two rivers – the Glaslyn and the Colwyn – meet near a picturesque old stone bridge in the centre of the village. For one of the most scenic drives in Snowdonia, take the A498 which follows the course of the Glaslyn north-eastwards past two idyllic lakes – Llyn Dinas and Llyn Gwynant – before climbing up the shoulder of the Nant Gwynant pass into the rocky heights of Snowdonia.

Beddgelert is in the midst of magnificent walking country. The poet William Wordsworth set off on a dawn ascent of Snowdon from here. But in addition to challenging mountain terrain there are gentle woodland walks amongst the conifers of the Beddgelert forest to the north and along the track of the old Welsh Highland Railway to the south.

The railway once travelled through one of North Wales's most famous beauty spots, the Aberglaslyn pass, where the Glaslyn forces its way through a narrow, gloomy defile flanked by sheer cliffs. Although Beddgelert and the Aberglaslyn pass give the impression of being locked in by the mountains, the village is only 7 miles from the sea. It comes as a surprise to discover that the Glaslyn was once a tidal river, allowing ships to sail all the way to the much-photographed bridge at the southern entrance to the pass.

Nearby
Cae Du Farm Park (off A498 on north-eastern approach to village). Tel (076686) 345. C. Working farm beside river Glaslyn. 1½-mile walk around farmlands with many animals and birds.

Sygun Copper Mine (off A498 1 mile north-east of Beddgelert). Tel (076686) 595. C. Conducted tours of old mine which recreates the world of the Victorian miner. Winding tunnels contain ore veins, stalactites and stalagmites.

Beddgelert, one of Snowdonia's prettiest villages

BENLLECH

GWYNEDD **C2**

You'll have more than enough sand to yourself at Benllech

Benllech is a popular holiday centre on the eastern shores of the Isle of Anglesey. A beautiful, golden-sanded beach backed by cliffs extends southwards from a holiday village whose charms have not been swamped by excessive commercialism.

Around the headland there are more sands – 10 square miles in all at low tide – along Traeth Coch, otherwise known as Red Wharf Bay. The few dwellings which make up the settlement of Red Wharf Bay look out across a vast expanse of sheltered sands fringed by rock pools and green, wooded hills. Walkers on these sands should be wary of the tides.

Nearby
Rhuddlan Fawr Open Farm, Brynteg (off B5110 about 2¹/₂ miles south-west of Benllech). Tel (0248) 852216. C. Small farm museum with bygone items. Waymarked trail through farmlands.

BETHESDA

GWYNEDD **C3**

The old slate town of Bethesda lies at the foot of the Nant Ffrancon pass. Man-made phenomena compete with Snowdonia's natural grandeur for attention at sombre Bethesda, whose slopes bear the gouges created by the world's largest opencast slate quarry. From here, the slate was transported a short distance to the sea at Port Penrhyn, Bangor.

Travel in the other direction and you enter a world of rugged beauty, misty heights and jagged peaks. The Nant Ffrancon pass climbs up into this desolate wilderness. The route was described as 'the most dreadful horse path in Wales' before Thomas Telford came along and took advantage of the natural break in the mountains to lay his road – now the A5 – to Holyhead.

The pass lies sandwiched between two of Snowdonia's most spectacular mountain ranges. The uplands to the east of the road are filled with the Carneddau, the collective name for Wales's second-highest mountains. Snowdonia's raw, elemental personality is nowhere stronger than amongst the peaks of Carnedd Dafydd at 1044m (3424ft) and Carnedd Llywelyn at 1066m (3485ft), two summits named after medieval Welsh nobility.

On the opposite side of the road are the Glyders, a boulder-strewn range with the primeval qualities of a lost world. The most celebrated peak here is Tryfan; although a mere 917m (3010 ft), this fierce, volcanic outcrop is possibly the most challenging summit in the whole of North Wales. This was the region in which the first successful Everest expedition trained in the early 1950s (the names of team members are written on the ceiling of the Pen-y-Gwryd Inn, a famous mountain hostelry on the A4086 south-west of Capel Curig).

Tryfan, in the mountains above Bethesda

Tryfan rises abruptly above the roadside and lake of Llyn Ogwen. Llyn Idwal, accessible by path from the road, is hidden away within Cwm Idwal (the area surrounding the lake is a national nature reserve, the first to be created in Wales). The dark, rocky outcrop above its waters is known as Twll Du (the 'Black Hole' or Devil's Kitchen) where, according to legend, no bird ever flies. Don't be put off by one 18th-century travel writer who was sufficiently intimidated by these surroundings to describe them as 'a fit place to inspire murderous thought, environed with horrible precipices, shading a lake'.

Joys of Life Visitor Centre. Tel (0248) 602122. C. A wide range of hobby items and mementos on display, including railwayana, models, old toys, radios old and new. Centre also has quarryman's kitchen and aircraft relics.

Paths and forest trails lead into the wooded slopes above Betws-y-coed

Betws-y-coed is built almost entirely of stone quarried in the mountains of Gwynedd. This brings it into perfect harmony with its dramatic setting in a steep valley, hemmed in by forested slopes. Much-mispronounced Betws-y-coed is the Welsh mountain resort that everyone has heard of. The village became a holiday centre with the arrival of the railway in 1868. The vogue for travel in Victorian times brought visitors streaming into the area. Grand hotels sprang up, many of which still thrive today.

It is a favourite haunt all year round of those who love the outdoor life. Naturalists, ramblers, anglers, artists and photographers can be seen any day gathered at the village's heart, the famous Pont-y-Pair (Bridge of the Cauldron), named thus because, after heavy rains, raging floodwaters crash down into a pool beneath.

Waymarked routes into the surrounding mountains and forests lead out of the village from Pont-y-Pair. Amongst the most popular are those to the Miner's Bridge, the Fairy Glen and Conwy Falls,

Swallow Falls and Tŷ Hyll (The Ugly House). Many of these paths were used by lead miners who laboured in mines such as the old workings to be found half-way up the public footpath to the lake of Llyn y Parc. Until the days of widespread car ownership, the wives of local farmers and forest workers struggled up this same pathway laden with shopping baskets on their way home from the market in Llanrwst.

Three rivers, the Conwy, Llugwy and Lledr, meet in the valley and all three enjoy a fine reputation for good runs of salmon and sewin (sea-trout). Coraclemen once fished these waters, especially at night, when they would draw their nets across the river before drifting silently downstream to trap the unsuspecting fish.

A fine stone building, once the stables of the Royal Oak Hotel, houses an excellent visitor centre. Well-designed displays provide information on local history, farming, folklore and wildlife, as well as the Snowdonia National Park and surrounding Gwydyr forest. You can explore the forest on tours from the centre accompanied by guides expert in the local flora and fauna.

Railway enthusiasts, young and old, will find the Railway Museum with its fleet of working model railways and miniature steam trains irresistible. The nearby Motor Museum is popular too. It contains a collection of vintage and post-vintage thoroughbred cars with some rare examples, including the Bugatti Type 57.

There are a number of old and fascinating bridges in the district. West of the incomparable Pont-y-Pair lies the Miner's Bridge which was built by the old-time lead miners on the line of a Roman road, while to the south, crossing the river Conwy, is Beaver Bridge, dating from 1800. Perhaps the most interesting structure is Waterloo Bridge, an iron bridge designed and built by Thomas Telford to carry the A5 across the river Conwy. Prominently inscribed in cast iron and covering the full length of the span on both sides is the message, 'This arch was constructed in the same year the battle of

Swallow Falls, a famous North Wales beauty spot

Waterloo was fought'. National emblems of England, Ireland, Scotland and Wales complete the decoration of the arch.

Two special attractions lie within easy reach of the village. The first is Swallow Falls, 2 miles west beside the A5. This tumultuous waterfall, pouring into a deep ravine, has been acclaimed since Victorian times. A little further along the road is one of the strangest looking houses in the British Isles. Tŷ Hyll (The Ugly House) appears to have been constructed by giants who piled huge boulders haphazardly together.

Exhibition and Visitor Centre. Tel (0690) 710426. F. Information on Snowdonia National Park. Gwydyr forest interpretive display. Children's Wildlife Tunnel. Royal Society for the Protection of Birds display. 'Living Water' exhibition (C) within centre contains live freshwater and sea creatures.

Motor Museum. Tel (0690) 710632/710427. C. Exotic and vintage cars.

Railway Museum. Tel (0690) 710568. C. Displays and a miniature railway. Buffet car. Picnic area.

Nearby
Swallow Falls. Tel (0690) 710796. C. One of North Wales's most famous beauty spots.

Tŷ Hyll (The Ugly House). Tel (06904) 287. C. Looks like something out of a Grimms' fairytale.

BLAENAU FFESTINIOG
GWYNEDD   D4

On the northern approach to Blaenau Ffestiniog, the landscape of heather-covered mountains switches abruptly to a stark grey. The legacy of a once-thriving slate industry is all around Blaenau. Slate brought the town its prosperity in the 19th century, transforming it from a scattered community of hill farms to a major industrial centre, the 'slate capital of North Wales'.

Slate has now turned it into a living museum. The industry began to wane in the 1960s, but even at its height, most of the wealth was enjoyed by a few powerful 'slate barons'. Blaenau's quarries have a long history of conflict and hardship; today they have become fascinating centres of industrial history, though their slate mountains still tower over the town, jagged and gleaming when dampened with a veneer of rain.

Despite the ever-present evidence of slate, Blaenau enjoys a ruggedly beautiful setting in the Vale of Ffestiniog, between the craggy Moelwyn and Manod mountain ranges. The narrow-gauge railway which once carried slate to Porthmadog is now a popular attraction, taking tourists on a 65-minute journey through the majestic scenery of the Snowdonia National Park. Tourism has brought new life to the town, making up for the loss of revenue and population which followed the declining demand for slate.

The Llechwedd Slate Caverns opened to visitors in 1972 and a trip into the chambers by electric train gives a vivid idea of the skill and courage needed for a mining life. Other features here include a Deep Mine tour, Slate Heritage Theatre and tram exhibition. Llechwedd's example was followed by Gloddfa Ganol, the world's biggest slate mine, where you can see three quarrymen's cottages, furnished to show changing lifestyles from the 1880s to 1945, and a locomotive museum which includes an engine well over 100 years old; and take a cold journey into the mine itself (wear warm clothes and good shoes). Half-lit tunnels, sound effects and echoing caverns make this a gripping experience.

Slate is everywhere in Blaenau, but now appears in shops as well as on roofs, carved into stylish and lasting gifts. Even the town's fountain is a solid pillar of slate. Economic revival has made Blaenau Ffestiniog a bustling, cheerful place, crowded with visitors in summer but still a distinctly Welsh community.

Gloddfa Ganol Mountain Centre

A mile into the mountains south of Blaenau, the Ffestiniog Hydro-electric Pump Storage Station provides tours to its top reservoir, where Stwlan Dam, 305m (1000ft) up, looks out towards the peaks of Snowdonia. Visitors can get there by car or minibus. An information centre on the lower level has a free exhibition explaining how electricity is made from water power. The Ffestiniog Railway has a station at Tan-y-Grisiau for access to the power station.

Ffestiniog Railway. Tel (0766) 831654. C. Scenic 13¹/₂-mile journey through Snowdonia National Park to railway's main terminus at Porthmadog.

Gloddfa Ganol Mountain Centre. Tel (0766) 830664. C. Locomotive display, quarrymen's cottages and museum. Watch craftsmen splitting slate and walk into mountain passages and caverns.

Llechwedd Slate Caverns. Tel (0766) 830306. C. Two tours available – the Miners' Tramway into the side of the mountain and Deep Mine down Britain's steepest passenger incline railway. Theatre and tram exhibition.

Nearby
Ffestiniog Pumped Storage Power Station, Tan-y-Grisiau. Tel (0766) 830310. F but C for tours. Display on hydro-electricity and tours of top reservoir.

MARKET DAYS

The country comes to town on market day. If you want to experience the bustle and atmosphere of a Welsh market, then plan your visit from the list below. Market days are great social as well as commercial occasions – it's the day in the week when farming folk not only buy and sell livestock, but also catch up on the local gossip.

Sheep sales at Ruthin

LIVESTOCK MARKETS

Abergele	Monday (weekly)
Bala	Thursday (weekly)
Bryncir	Tuesday (weekly)
Corwen	Tuesday (weekly)
Denbigh	Tuesday & Friday (weekly)
Llangefni	Wednesday & Thursday (weekly)
Llanrwst	Wednesday & Friday (weekly)
Mold	Monday, Wednesday & Friday (weekly)
Pwllheli	Monday (weekly) & Saturday (occasional)
Ruthin	Friday (weekly)
St Asaph	Thursday (weekly)
Valley	Monday (monthly)
Wrexham	Monday (weekly)

GENERAL MARKETS

There are also many weekly general markets held throughout North Wales, where stallholders set up shop either under cover or in the streets. Some coincide with livestock markets.

Abergele	Friday, Saturday & Sunday
Amlwch	Friday

Bangor	Friday & Saturday
Caernarfon	Saturday
Colwyn Bay	Tuesday & Saturday
Connah's Quay	Thursday
Conwy	Saturday & Tuesday (summer)
Denbigh	Wednesday
Flint	Thursday
Holyhead	Friday & Saturday
Holywell	Thursday & Saturday
Llangefni	Thursday
Llangollen	Tuesday
Llanrwst	Tuesday
Mold	Wednesday & Saturday
Prestatyn	Tuesday & Friday
Pwllheli	Wednesday
Rhyl	Monday, Thursday & Saturday
Ruthin	First Tuesday every month

AN EVENTFUL PLACE

Wales is an eventful place. A full and lively programme of events takes place throughout the year – there's everything from music festivals to medieval pageants, guided walks to country fairs. In a guide of this size, it's impossible to mention them all, or to give specific dates. Please call in at a Tourist Information Centre for the full picture.

We have made brief reference to selected important events under the relevant locations in the gazetteer. Wales's three major annual events are the Llangollen International Musical Eisteddfod, which takes place for a week in the first part of July, the Royal Welsh Agricultural Show, held in Builth Wells, Mid Wales, for four days in late July, and the week-long Royal National Eisteddfod, held at a different location each year in the first part of August.

The colourful, cosmopolitan Llangollen International Eisteddfod

17

BODEDERN

GWYNEDD   **B2**

Sleepy Bodedern stands amongst the Isle of Anglesey's flat, fertile farmlands. Anglesey's agriculture, arable and pastoral, is the theme of Farm Life, a visitor attraction based on a working farm south of the village. Traditional whitewashed farm buildings and barns ranged around a farmyard contain a milking parlour, hatchery, livestock pens, pets' corner and farm equipment display. An old farmhouse kitchen, complete with stone-flagged floors and open fireplace, gives visitors a glimpse into the lifestyle of bygone times.

The Presaddfed Burial Chamber – it should be plural, for there are two small prehistoric tombs here – stands in farmland nearly a mile north-east of Bodedern.

Nearby
Farm Life (off minor road about 1 mile south-west of Bodedern). Tel (0407) 741171. C. Presents authentic view of a working farm. Children's adventure playground, picnic area.

BODELWYDDAN

CLWYD   **E2**

The beautiful castle of Bodelwyddan has become one of the most important attractions in North Wales. As a provincial outpost of the National Portrait Gallery it houses a magnificent collection of 19th-century portraits and photographs, and has been praised for the authenticity of its opulent Victorian interiors.

The atmosphere of the restored walled garden is enchanting. In addition to a host of exotic plants and shrubs it contains a Victorian-style aviary filled with species popular in the 19th century. There's something for all the family here – the children will enjoy an adventure woodland and toddlers' play

Victorian splendour at Bodelwyddan

area, leaving parents free to lay out picnics in the castle's grand surroundings.

A mile away, in Bodelwyddan itself, is a building of locally quarried limestone which surpasses even the castle in its stunning visual effect. In bright sunlight the 19th-century 'Marble' Church, with its shining white spire and marble arcades, is a vision of splendour equalled by few ecclesiastical buildings in Britain.

Bodelwyddan Castle (off A55). Tel (0745) 584060. C. National Portrait Gallery exhibition. Period furniture and sculpture. Cultural events throughout summer months.

BRYNSIENCYN

GWYNEDD   **C3**

The fields around this Isle of Anglesey village have witnessed human settlement for many thousands of years. The Bodowyr Burial Chamber, a small tomb probably of the neolithic (New Stone Age) period, stands amongst farmland 1¼ miles north-west of the village. Along the same road out of the village is

Bodelwyddan Castle, home of an outstanding art collection

Caer Lêb, a substantial earthwork enclosure 61m (200ft) long by 49m (160ft) wide. Excavations, which have revealed a brooch, Roman coin and pottery, indicate that it was inhabited in the 3rd and 4th centuries AD.

But Brynsiencyn is on the tourist map not because of its historic sites. The village is now well known as the home of the Anglesey Sea Zoo, one of a new breed of attractions in North Wales. The zoo is located a mile or so south-west of the village on the banks of the Menai Strait. This highly successful, award-winning attraction presents sea creatures large and small in an imaginative way. Visitors can walk through a simulated undersea 'shipwreck' area, watch the ebb and flow of the tides in a 'tides tank' and even touch some of the zoo's inhabitants.

From the Anglesey Sea Zoo, it's worth continuing along the coast road as far as it goes. From the end of the road, almost opposite Caernarfon, there are magnificent views across the Menai Strait to mighty Caernarfon Castle and the mountains of Snowdonia beyond.

Anglesey Sea Zoo (on minor road 1¼ miles south-west of Brynsiencyn). Tel (0248) 430411/430412. C. Popular family attraction. Sea creatures, water game, children's playboat, trout farm.

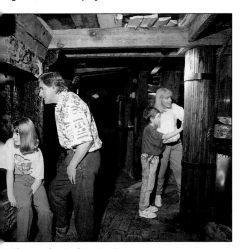

The popular Anglesey Sea Zoo

CAERGWRLE

CLWYD   F3

Dafydd, brother of Llywelyn ap Gruffudd, Llywelyn the Last, began building Caergwrle Castle in 1278. Four years later, when Edward I and his queen were in residence, the castle was destroyed by a disastrous fire. Since no repairs were ever made later travellers discovered, 'only a place ... whose walls and towers are largely thrown down'. This remains an apt description of the poor ruin we see today.

Caergwrle Castle. F. Medieval border fortress, now a hilltop ruin.

CAERNARFON

GWYNEDD   C3

Caernarfon Castle was built as a symbol of English power after the defeat of the native Welsh prince Llywelyn the Last by Edward I in 1283. Today its lofty turrets still tower over a town which has lost none of its Welsh character. Caernarfon's historic significance has turned it into a major North Wales centre. Although the medieval castle is the main attraction, the town's military roots go back much further. The Romans built a fort here known as *Segontium* in about AD78, the excavated ruins of which are now open to the public together with a museum displaying some of the many finds discovered on site.

But most visitors to Caernarfon first explore the castle and its immediate surroundings. The main shopping streets wind their way around sturdy 13th-century town walls, a further mark of Edward I's conquest and control, for the king founded at Caernarfon not only a castle but a complete medieval township. A busy Saturday market takes place in Y Maes, on the castle's front doorstep. And on this square, where, according to tradition, Edward presented his first-born son as the Prince of Wales, stands a statue of a local MP who became one of Britain's most renowned Prime Ministers – David Lloyd George.

The investiture of the current Prince of Wales, Prince Charles, took place at Caernarfon in 1969 and an exhibition in the castle's north-east tower traces the history of the royal title back to its only Welsh holder, Llywelyn ap Gruffudd, Llywelyn the Last, recognized as prince in 1267. From the top of the castle walls you can view the harbour with its swing-bridge and forest of yacht masts; and in the Queen's Tower the Regimental Museum of the Royal Welch Fusiliers contains military exhibits, including a 7kg (16lb) Russian cannon, which tell the story of Wales's oldest infantry regiment. Further exhibitions, on

Fireworks at Caernarfon

various historical themes, can be seen in other towers, together with an audio-visual display. Down on the harbour, the little Maritime Museum features a steam-powered dredger, SS *Seiont II*, built in 1937 and now owned by the National Museum of Wales.

In Cwrt Llywelyn, a small square opposite the castle, the arched modern offices of Gwynedd County Council blend in well with Caernarfon's medieval buildings. A striking slate sculpture here commemorates the death of Llywelyn in 1282; its representation of a white eagle was inspired by the prince's title Eryr Eryrod Eryri (The Eagle of Eagles of Snowdonia).

A few miles to the south-west, just off the A499, is Parc Glynllifon, near the turn-off to Dinas Dinlle and the Caernarfon Air World (see Dinas Dinlle entry for details of the two attractions).

Caernarfon Castle. Tel (0286) 77617. C (includes entry to Regimental Museum, audio-visual presentation and exhibitions). Wales's most famous castle and a World Heritage Listed Site. Designed to serve as a royal palace and seat of government as well as a military stronghold. ✢

Maritime Museum, Victoria Dock. Tel (0286) 2118. C. Exhibition traces shipping history of Caernarfon and Menai Strait; ex-dredger, tied up at dock, forms part of museum.

Segontium Roman Fort and Museum, Beddgelert Road. Tel (0286) 5625. F. Excavations reveal layout of fort. Small display shows documents, weapons and uniforms of the Roman occupiers and explains their history. ✢ 🏛

CAERWYS

CLWYD   E3

This small, peaceful village lies at the northern end of the Clwydian Range. Its orderly grid-pattern layout harks back to the time of its creation and role as a medieval borough and important market town (although diminished in size and status over the years, it is still officially a town). Perhaps something of Caerwys's urban planning found its way to America, for Dr Thomas Wynne, a native of the town, was instrumental in planning the layout of Philadelphia.

Caerwys has long links with the traditions of the eisteddfod. In 1568, Elizabeth 1 granted permission for 20 'gentlemen of North Wales' to call together bards and minstrels for a national cultural gathering, an event which is seen as marking the revival of the eisteddfod in Wales. The occasion is commemorated by a window in St Michael's Church.

Mighty Caernarfon Castle, the best known of Wales's many medieval fortresses

Snowdon and its neighbouring peaks from Llynnau Mymbyr

CAPEL CURIG

GWYNEDD   D3

This mountain village, which stands amidst Snowdonia's highest peaks, is the spiritual home of many an outdoor enthusiast. Tryfan, the Glyders and the Carneddau are all close by (see Bethesda entry), Moel Siabod rears up 872m (2861ft) to the south-west, while the majestic 1085m (3560ft) summit of Snowdon itself – the highest point in England and Wales – dominates the western skyline 7 miles away.

The villages stands at the gateway to the Nant Ffrancon and Llanberis passes. Follow the A4086 towards Pen-y-Gwryd past the twin lakes of Llynnau Mymbyr for one of the classic views in North Wales – the mighty 'horseshoe' made up of Snowdon and its neighbouring peaks. There is an outdoor pursuits centre on the outskirts of the village.

CEMAES BAY

GWYNEDD   B2

The rocky coastline around Cemaes Bay, on the distant northern shores of the Isle of Anglesey, is a place of unexpected contrasts. Much of the coast here is in the care of the National Trust; the unexpected element takes the form of a large complex, the Wylfa Nuclear Power Station, perched on an otherwise undeveloped shoreline.

Cemaes Bay itself, the most northerly village in Wales, is an exceptionally pretty place. A perfect crescent of sands leads to an old stone quay lined with fishing boats and holiday craft moored in still, sheltered waters. A mile or so to the west is Cemlyn Bay, another lovely expanse of coastline. A long spit of land separates the sea from a lagoon-like lake with a nature reserve along its shores. This stretch of water, almost landlocked by the pebble-backed spit, is now a major bird sanctuary particularly noted for its colony of terns.

The headland church at Llanbadrig overlooking the eastern entrance to Cemaes Bay is an ancient place of worship. It is said to be the only church in Wales dedicated to St Patrick, Ireland's patron saint.

Wylfa Nuclear Power Station. Tel (0407) 710471. F. Guided tours of the largest and most advanced power station of its type in the world. Information centre, cinema, exhibition.

A curving shore protects picturesque Cemaes Bay from the open seas

CERRIGYDRUDION

CLWYD   E4

From Cerrigydrudion the eye is held by wide expanses of bare moorland and cloud-capped hilltops silhouetted on distant horizons. Here and there clumps of woodland, planted for shelter, indicate the site of an upland sheep farm. In all this vast landscape only the hardy Welsh mountain sheep stir, patiently searching for scant grazing.

The development of nearby Llyn Brenig (see entry) as a popular outdoor recreation centre has opened up the village's tourist potential. Nowadays, walkers and fishermen requiring accommodation near to the lake stay here in increasing numbers.

21

SNOWDONIA NATIONAL PARK

Llyn Gwynant, in Snowdon's foothills

Ogwen Falls, Nant Ffrancon pass

This 840-square-mile national park takes its name from the highest mountain range in England and Wales. The 1085m (3560ft) peak of Snowdon, a jagged pinnacle, is the focal point of the north-western corner of the park. This is the magnet that attracts thousands of walkers and outdoor enthusiasts each year. Yet there is more – much more – to this national park than the Snowdonia range, pre-eminent though it is. The park covers a great deal of Mid as well as North Wales; in this sense, its name is deceptive, for the Snowdonia National Park's extensive boundaries stretch eastwards as far as Bala and southwards all the way to Machynlleth.

In North Wales, however, there's nothing ambiguous about the park's dominant feature. Almost every perspective has the backdrop of a serrated skyline carved by the razor-sharp ridges of Snowdon and its neighbouring peaks. The roll-call of challenging mountains – Tryfan, the Glyders, the Carneddau – is on the lips of all self-respecting outdoor enthusiasts. This was the territory which first attracted intrepid Victorian walkers. This was the territory in which the team trained for the first successful attempt on Mount Everest. And this was the territory which served as the proving ground for trail-blazing British climbers such as Joe Brown.

Scenic variety has always been Snowdonia's strong point, even in the mountainous north. Snowdon itself, for example, is only 10 miles from the sea; and the lower lands around the mountains consist of wooded valleys, open moors, lakes, rivers, forests and waterfalls. To experience the contrasting sides of Snowdonia, go first to Llanberis at the foot of Snowdon (this is a good walking centre from which to venture into the high ground). Then visit Betws-y-coed, which is surrounded by a gentler landscape of wooded hillsides which can be explored on a network of easy-to-follow waymarked walks.

The national park runs a series of guided walks throughout the year, and has a residential study centre at Plas Tan-y-Bwlch, Maentwrog, Gwynedd (tel 0766-85324). Call in for further details on all aspects of the park at information centres in Bala, Betws-y-coed, Blaenau Ffestiniog and Llanberis.

Rugged, rocky heights, typical Snowdonia territory

Chirk Castle

CHIRK
CLWYD   F4

Chirk's famous Marcher castle was constructed in the late 13th century on behalf of Edward 1 who was determined to hold his Welsh conquests at any cost. The description 'castle' is perhaps a misnomer, for Chirk, now in the care of the National Trust, has evolved over the centuries into a comfortable stately home. It stands in a strategic position commanding the English-Welsh border, the only 13th-century English castle in Wales to have been in continuous occupation since it was built. The Myddleton family of Chirk owned the castle from 1595, a fact which, in spite of the grimness of its squat walls and towers, accounts for the interior's homely, stylish atmosphere.

A central courtyard reflects architectural styles spanning 400 years. Memorable features include displays of weapons and firearms in the Cromwell Hall, the Long Gallery and the treasures of the state rooms. Beneath Adam's Tower is an exceptionally hideous dungeon ventilated only by two tiny slits in walls 4¹/₂m (15ft) thick.

On leaving the dungeon it is a relief to walk in the castle grounds where a beautiful garden, containing rare shrubs and magnificent specimen trees, complements the grandeur of this splendid castle.

Chirk Castle. Tel (0691) 777701. C. Mansion which developed from border fortress. Magnificent entrance gates. 🦋

Nearby
Tŷ Mawr Country Park, Cae Gwilym Road, Cefn-mawr. Tel (0978) 822780. F. In Dee valley. Riverside walks, animals, picnic areas, ranger service.

CILCAIN
CLWYD   F3

Cilcain is locked away in the maze of hills and valleys which lie on the eastern slopes of the Clwydian Range. Nothing disturbs the peace of this rural backwater unless you would object to the bleating of Welsh mountain sheep grazing in the shadow of the parish church – itself a timeless symbol of the seemingly unspoiled serenity of this corner of North Wales. Moel Fammau, at 555m (1821ft) the highest point on the range, overshadows the village. Weary walkers find rest and refreshment at Cilcain's picturesque 16th-century inn.

CLYNNOG FAWR
GWYNEDD   B4

The cottages of Clynnog Fawr are dwarfed by a vast 16th-century church more reminiscent of an Oxford college than a hamlet on the Llŷn peninsula. A long tradition of worship and pilgrimage began here with the founding of the original church by St Beuno in AD630. Pilgrims on their way to Bardsey island, the 'Island of 20,000 Saints', brought in a steady revenue in the Middle Ages and funded the building of the present church, which has an impressive carved rood screen and ceiling. The choir stalls and misericords, dating from about 1500, are the finest in the county. A medieval chest, hollowed out of one piece of wood and on display near the porch, once held the parish records and charitable offerings. A chapel next to the belltower houses St Beuno's Stone, dating from between the 7th and 9th centuries and probably used either as a boundary marker or as a prayer stone. A well dedicated to the saint is located a few hundred metres from the church.

Clynnog Fawr sits beneath the triple peaks of Yr Eifl (often anglicized to 'The Rivals'), overlooking the sea. There is a pebble beach, with sand at low tide, at Aberdesach, a mile up the road towards Caernarfon. The Museum of Welsh Country Life is well signposted on a road leading into the mountains above the village, with far-reaching views of the coast. At the museum, housed in a 17th-century watermill, everyday items illustrate the domestic and working life of rural Wales.

Nearby
Museum of Welsh Country Life, Felin Faesog, Tai'r Lon. Tel (0286) 86311. C. Clothes, tools and domestic memorabilia, including hand-sewn nightdresses and a sand toilet.

Meet the chimps at the Welsh Mountain Zoo

COLWYN BAY
CLWYD   D2

Colwyn Bay lies on a sandy coastline overlooked by wooded green hills leading to some of Wales's most beautiful countryside. The town's popularity as a seaside resort developed late in the 19th century. Much of its old-established and comfortable atmosphere derives from the distinctive Victorian architecture of many of its private dwellings and public buildings.

There is much to see along the resort's superb 3-mile promenade. Waterskiers continually skim by; yachts tack and often capsize; windsurfers fly like gulls over the whitecaps. This long seafront walkway runs into neighbouring Rhos on Sea, whose newly constructed breakwater has created a little harbour with an atmosphere akin to that of a West Wales coastal village.

Eirias Park, the 'park by the sea', contains a boating lake, picnic area, tennis, bowling, children's playground, amusements and the Dinosaur World attraction, where 30 life-size model dinosaurs 'roam' in a mock-prehistoric environment. The park is also the home of an athletics track and the Colwyn Leisure Centre, a multi-purpose sports complex with a superb indoor leisure pool.

Two theatres provide light entertainment. The Harlequin Puppet Theatre at Rhos on Sea, one of the few of its kind in Britain, delights parents and children alike. The Prince of Wales Theatre, Abergele Road, with its constantly changing programme of colourful summer shows, is equally popular.

Colwyn Bay is good for shopping, with the focus on the town's new glass-vaulted mall known as the Colwyn Centre. Behind the town lies Pwllycrochan Woods, a belt of mature woodland popular as a nature trail and silent refuge from the frenetic bustle of the seaside.

From Pwllycrochan it is a short step to the Welsh Mountain Zoo, the resort's most celebrated attraction. In addition to the lure of wild animals caged in natural surroundings, skilfully managed flying displays featuring sea-eagles have always thrilled large crowds. Even these favourites have recently been upstaged by the creation of Chimpanzee World, in which up to 20 resident chimps amuse audiences by their behaviour. The zoo's elevated position presents visitors with views of magnificent, untouched countryside waiting to be explored just a few miles inland.

Eirias Park, Promenade. Tel (0492) 533223/4. F. Leisure park and sports complex within park-like surrounds. Includes: Leisure Centre. Tel (0492) 533223/4. C; Dinosaur World. Tel (0492) 518111. C.

Harlequin Puppet Theatre, Cayley Promenade, Rhos on Sea. Tel (0492) 48166. Matinée and evening puppet shows.

Prince of Wales Theatre, Abergele Road. Tel (0492) 532668. Various productions all year.

Welsh Mountain Zoo, Llanrwst Road. Tel (0492) 532938. C. Outstanding zoo in outstanding location. Free minibus service from Colwyn Bay Station to the zoo.

Conwy's situation on the wooded banks of a broad estuary in the shadow of Snowdonia's mountains is magnificent. But the first impression to strike visitors is the way in which the town's past and present are inextricably intertwined. The battered hulk of a mighty 13th-century castle presides from its perch above the estuary, a brooding stronghold which throws out a ring of ancient town walls which still effectively encircles the central core of Conwy.

When Edward I finally conquered Snowdonia in 1283, he decided to establish his power over the rebellious Welsh princes by constructing a series of massive stone fortresses. Conwy was a site of such obvious strategic importance that, within days of his arrival, the king had issued orders for the building to begin. The task of completion was considered so urgent that armies of craftsmen and labourers were brought here from every part of England. An incredible feat of industry and organization resulted in the castle and town walls being completed by the autumn of 1287.

The castle's last military engagement was fought during the Civil War. In 1646 after a three-month siege it fell to Cromwell's forces. At the Restoration the Earl of Conwy became its owner and immediately set about stripping the castle of its iron, timber and lead. Despite the centuries of ruinous decline which followed, the castle, whose slim, semicircular towers look from afar like a vision of Camelot, still remains one of Europe's outstanding examples of military architecture. It has been designated a World Heritage Listed Site, and is the best place from which to begin an exploration of the town.

Enjoy a bird's-eye view from Conwy's lofty turrets

The craggy town walls, looping down from the battlements like a protective arm, enclose most of Conwy ancient and modern. At one time they completely encircled the town in the shape of a self-contained citadel. Today, visitors can still walk along sections of the walls and enjoy commanding views across the rooftops of the town towards the estuary and castle.

A foray into Conwy awakens echoes of 800 years of history, reflected in the unchanging pattern of streets and in the strongly medieval atmosphere of three important buildings. The 14th-century Church of St Mary and All Saints occupies the site of the former 12th-century Cistercian Abbey of Aberconwy. Parts of its walls date from 1190. A holy water stoup, predating the Reformation, in which worshippers would dip their hands to bless themselves, stands in a niche inside the door.

On the corner of Castle Street is Aberconwy House, a gracious stone-and-timber building dating from the 14th century. It was once the home of a prosperous Conwy merchant. The first floor highlights Conwy's links with the sea, particularly the mussel fishing industry. Second-floor panels depict the town's history and are enlivened by 'The Conwy Story' on video.

The 16th-century mansion of Plas Mawr is currently the home of the Royal Cambrian Academy of Art (which is due to move next door to Seion Chapel). The house was built by Robert Wynne, a true Elizabethan adventurer. Cavernous fireplaces, stone-flagged floors, a haunted room, secret hiding places and a spacious banqueting hall make the house fascinating to explore. Many rooms and ceilings still retain their original decorative plasterwork of heraldic symbols and mythological

See if you can squeeze into the Smallest House

caulking boats or stowing fishing gear for an expedition to catch sea bass or the tasty Conwy dabs. Fishing has been an industry in Conwy since the town began and crowds always gather to watch trawlermen landing their catch.

On the same quay near the lifeboat station is the embarkation point for cruises up the estuary. Nearby is a sea and freshwater fish aquarium. Further along is the unbelievable Smallest House, a quayside curiosity measuring 3m (9ft) high by 1.8m (5ft) wide, the tiniest dwelling in Britain.

Beyond the quay the scenic Marine Walk follows the riverbank towards the open sea. From here visitors can cut across Bodlondeb Gardens to reach the Conwy Butterfly House where butterflies can be seen in all stages from egg to free-flying adults.

Conwy is at its liveliest in late July when the town holds its annual week-long festival.

creatures. Over the fireplace in the Queen's Room the royal coat-of-arms and the queen's initials 'E' and 'R' add to the house's Tudor atmosphere.

Until Thomas Telford's graceful suspension bridge was built in 1826 – notice the way in which its architecture mirrors that of the castle – Conwy could be reached from the estuary's east bank only by ferry. Telford built an embankment linking the east shore to an island in the river and then joined the crossing with his elegant bridge which, though it appears frail beside the more modern railway and road bridges, was the main road-crossing as late as 1956. In recent years the bridge has been extensively restored by the National Trust and will be reopened to visitors, along with its tollhouse, in 1992.

More of Conwy's history is featured at the Guildhall which provides lectures on the subject specially for visitors. In Rosehill Street the Conwy Visitor Centre brings history to life for all the family through film and scenic displays. The centre also offers an introduction to the skill of brass rubbing.

A glimpse of sparkling blue water through a breach in the town walls draws visitors to the quayside. On a wide reach of busy water multi-coloured craft of all sizes bob on the tide and lean into a keen breeze carrying the smell of the sea. The waterfront is a hive of activity; people rigging sails,

Aberconwy House. Tel (0492) 592246. C. Oldest surviving example of 14th-century Conwy merchant's house. 🦋

Conwy Aquarium. Tel (0492) 592366. C. On quayside.

Conwy Butterfly House, Bodlondeb Gardens. Tel (0492) 593149. C. Walk through a colourful 'jungle' environment containing butterflies, tropical birds and exotic plants.

Conwy Castle. Tel (0492) 592358. C. Evokes an authentic medieval spirit. Wonderful views from the towers. Study a detailed explanation of the castle's history at the visitor centre before entering the castle proper. ✿

Conwy Suspension Bridge. Telford's elegant bridge, opened 1826. Bridge and tollhouse closed for restoration until 1992. 🦋

Conwy Visitor Centre, Rosehill Street. Tel (0492) 596288. C. Film theatre, exhibition, craft and book shop. Brass rubbings.

Plas Mawr, High Street. Tel (0492) 593413. C. Elizabethan mansion with impressive period interior.

Smallest House, Quayside. C. Britain's smallest house furnished as a mid-Victorian Welsh cottage.

Conwy's defences loom above the waters of the estuary

Criccieth's headland castle commands superb views

CORWEN
CLWYD   E4

This old market town stands in pleasant surroundings above the river Dee at the entrance to the Vale of Edeyrnion. Fishing and hill walking are popular pastimes with visitors to these parts – the great bulk of the Berwyn mountains, an inviolate wilderness, rises to the south. Corwen is also a good place from which to explore the 'Glyndŵr Country' of Northeast Wales. Owain Glyndŵr, Wales's last native leader, led an uprising against English rule in the early 15th century. He has many associations locally. He took his name from his estate at Glyndyfrdwy, a village 4½ miles to the east of Corwen. Owain Glyndŵr's Mount, beside the A5 midway between Corwen and Glyndyfrdwy, is probably the site of his fortified manor.

Caer Derwyn, on the hill above the town to the north-east, is an Iron Age fort with well-preserved stone ramparts.

CRICCIETH
GWYNEDD   C4

Criccieth's roots as a Victorian seaside resort are evident in its gabled, bay-windowed villas and air of gentility. Its two beaches are separated by a prominent headland crowned by the ruined walls and ragged towers of Criccieth Castle. This fortress has seen plenty of action – in its time, it has been held by Welsh and English forces. The castle began life as a stronghold of the Welsh native princes. Following its capture and refortification by Edward 1 in 1283, it became a base of English power. Criccieth's fluctuating fortunes mirror those on the pages of Welsh history, for in 1404 it was captured and sacked by Owain Glyndŵr in Wales's last popular uprising against English authority.

The castle's twin-towered gatehouse survived the attentions of Glyndŵr's demolition experts. This formidable entranceway is easily the stronghold's most impressive feature, though the site itself – on a stubby peninsula with panoramic views overlooking Tremadog Bay – also merits admiration for its strong natural defences.

Criccieth is a picturesque, unassuming little seaside resort with a sand and shingle main beach which is popular with families. It's quite happy to go its own way catering for those who enjoy a quieter style of coastal holiday away from the razzmatazz of funfairs and flashing lights. The highlight of the summer season is the well-regarded Criccieth Festival, a music-based event.

Criccieth Castle. Tel (0766) 522227. C. A castle which, unusually, served both the Welsh and the English in its time. Contains an audio-visual presentation and exhibition. ✦

DENBIGH
CLWYD   E3

An impressive new Library Museum and Gallery, housed in the remodelled 16th-century County Hall, is the ideal centre from which to begin an exploration of historic Denbigh. This small but fascinating museum confirms the presence of prehistoric man at nearby Pontnewydd cave and contains rare funerary urns discovered at Bronze Age sites above Llyn Brenig (see Llyn Brenig entry). The history of the castle and its walled town are described in a detailed exhibition.

Henry de Lacy began building Denbigh Castle in 1282. The material used was locally quarried white limestone which, even today, gleams in the sunshine. The hilltop castle's most impressive military feature was its Great Gatehouse, formed by an elaborately planned interconnecting arrangement of three octagonal towers. Remains of the drawbridge pits, murder holes and portcullis grooves can still be seen.   *(contd overleaf)*

Historic Denbigh, in the fertile Vale of Clwyd

Before the battlements stands a solitary square tower, all that remains of the garrison church. The town walls, a section of which may be walked by arrangement with the castle's custodian, are also clearly visible from here. An unexpected bonus is the thrilling view of the whole length of the Clwydian Range, its series of softly moulded peaks winding towards the coast at Rhyl.

Denbigh's streets are filled with historical reminders. On Rhyl Road stands the House of the White Friars, another important 13th-century building. Near the castle is Leicester's Church or 'Leicester's Folly', an Elizabethan ruin built with the intention of replacing St Asaph's Cathedral. The community theatre is named after Twm o'r Nant, an 18th-century poet. Twm gained romantic notoriety because, when not working or composing, he filled in his spare time mugging those he disliked. Sir Henry Morton Stanley, the hero who found Dr Livingstone in deepest Africa, was born in a tiny cottage below the castle gatehouse. Behind the library is the Bull Hotel, a former coaching inn with a magnificent black-and-white, half-timbered exterior and, inside, a famous staircase stretching the full height of the building.

Denbigh Castle. Tel (0745) 813979. C. Hilltop fortress and town walls. An underrated site. ✣

Library Museum and Gallery, High Street. Tel (0745) 816313. F. Modern displays stimulate interest in the town's history and traditions.

DERWEN

CLWYD E3

Visit this village on the edge of the Hiraethog moorlands for its fascinating religious artefacts. The church, medieval in origin, has an elaborately carved rood screen and loft, together with old wall paintings. In the churchyard stands a stone cross, 'one of the finest in the Principality', carved with a Crucifixion and other figures.

Derwen Churchyard Cross. F. Well-preserved Celtic cross with fine carvings. ✣

DINAS DINLLE

GWYNEDD B3

The long, west-facing beach at Dinas Dinlle stands at the approach to a strange no-man's-land, a flat, dune-fringed promontory extending northwards to the Menai Strait's narrow western entrance. This wide, open area, an almost ready-made airfield, was used by the RAF during World War 11, and it was here that the first RAF mountain rescue team was formed. It is now the home of Caernarfon Airport and Caernarfon Air World. Beyond the airstrip stands Fort Belan (not open to the public), built at the tip of the promontory in the late 18th century to defend the western approach to the Menai Strait against the French.

Dinas Dinlle itself is a popular holiday spot with an excellent sandy beach, frequented by surfers and bass fishermen. From the sands there are superb views along the coast of the Llŷn peninsula to the Yr Eifl mountains.

Large-scale reconstruction has turned the grounds of Parc Glynllifon, at nearby Llandwrog, into a museum of cultural and working life. Machinery and mills have been cleaned and restored, and the Newborough Workshops allow visitors to sample life in a Victorian estate yard. Stately, Palladian Glynllifon Hall, the 19th-century home of the wealthy Newborough family, is a reminder of how the other half lived. A visitor centre is being developed to provide displays and refreshments, as well as demonstrations by contemporary craftspeople and artists. Woodland trails lead through the park, and there are formal gardens, unusual open-air sculptures, and an 18th-century fort.

Inside Caernarfon Air World

Caernarfon Air World. Tel (0286) 830800/831047. C. Air museum in huge, purpose-built hangar. Aeroplanes and helicopters, cockpits and controls with 'hands-on' experience, displays and cinema with aviation films. Also pleasure flights over Snowdon and Anglesey.

Nearby
Parc Glynllifon, Llandwrog (off A499). Tel (0286) 830222. Visitor Centre/Craft Workshops C; otherwise F. Park is being transformed into a major cultural centre. Nature trails, walk in/on sculptures, gardens, historic buildings, events.

ANGLESEY, LLŶN AND THE CLWYDIAN RANGE

South Stack, Anglesey's westernmost point

Ruthin lies beneath the open slopes of the Clwydian Range

Superb sands are a feature of the Llŷn peninsula

What do the Isle of Anglesey, Llŷn peninsula and the Clwydian Range have in common? All three are officially designated as being 'Areas of Outstanding Natural Beauty'. AONB status helps preserve and protect unspoilt coastline and countryside from the pressures of modern development. Anglesey's 125-mile coastline is a succession of sandy bays, sheltered inlets and rocky headlands dotted with small resorts – such as Moelfre and Trearddur Bay – whose subdued scale perfectly matches their surroundings.

Anglesey attracts those seeking quieter seaside holidays. There are beaches – the endless sands of Red Wharf Bay and Newborough, for instance – which never get crowded, even at the height of summer. And there are spectacular headlands – South Stack, near Holyhead is a supreme example – where you can spend the day admiring the view or watching the antics of colonies of sea-birds.

The Llŷn peninsula has an altogether more dramatic character. Go to its south-western tip – the 'Land's End' of North Wales – and gaze across the storm-tossed waters to Bardsey island. Or explore the exposed coastline around Porth Neigwl, otherwise known as Hell's Mouth.

Land and water meet savagely near Trefor on Llŷn's north-facing coast, where the mountains of Yr Eifl plunge almost vertically into the sea. The curtain of cliffs along this northern coast has only a few breaks where sandy bays have managed to squeeze

themselves in – the 'whistling sands' of Porth-oer, for example, and Nefyn's crescent-shaped beaches. Llŷn's more popular sands lie along its more sheltered southern shores, around Abersoch, Pwllheli and Criccieth.

The Clwydian Range, a long, rounded ridge of hills above the Vale of Clwyd, is the first upland barrier which many travellers encounter as they approach North Wales. The A494 from Mold to Ruthin loops through the southern section of the range, which rises to the 555m (1821ft) summit of Moel Fammau.

This is magnificent walking country, characterized by open hillsides, breezy heights and panoramic perspectives. The Offa's Dyke Footpath runs across this high ground, which commands views as far as the matchbox skyline of Liverpool to the east and the peaks of Snowdonia to the west.

Moelfre, on Anglesey's east coast

Dolwyddelan Castle, in the heart of Snowdonia

DOLWYDDELAN

GWYNEDD   **D3**

The single square tower of Dolwyddelan Castle, standing on a ridge above the valley floor, is a prominent sight for miles around. It was a castle of the Welsh native princes, built in the early 13th century by Llywelyn the Great to guard a mountain pass through Snowdonia. He chose the site well. Dolwyddelan's strategic importance was evident in the fact that, following the castle's fall to English forces in the troubled late 13th century, King Edward 1 promptly refortified the site for his own purposes.

There are marvellous views across to Moel Siabod from the restored Victorian battlements and wall-walks. The castle houses a small exhibition which tells the story of Dolwyddelan and other strongholds built by the Welsh.

The castle stands on the fringes of a peaceful village – an ideal walking or touring centre – surrounded by some of the wildest scenery in Snowdonia.

Dolwyddelan Castle. C. Lonely mountain stronghold of the native Welsh princes. ✵

DYSERTH

CLWYD   **E2**

A plunging 18m (60ft) waterfall marks the lowest point between the tiny villages of Upper and Lower Dyserth. 'Dissart' is recorded in the *Domesday Book* of 1086 as having 'a church with a priest, and 11 villeins, and a mill worth 11 shillings'. Henry III's castle, built in 1241, has been razed to the ground by mining. The parish church, parts of which date to the 13th century, contains 14th-century coffin lids, a

wheeled cross, and the 'Jesse' window saved from Basingwerk Abbey.

Close by is Bodrhyddan Hall, 17th-century home of Lord Langford, the Hereditary Constable of Rhuddlan Castle. Amongst items of note the hall contains paintings, armour, fine furniture and Egyptian relics which include a mummy. In addition to a formal French Garden, the grounds contain an octagonal well-house known as St Mary's Well. Dated 1612, it bears the name 'Inigo Jones'.

Bodrhyddan Hall (midway between Dyserth and Rhuddlan). Tel (0745) 590414. C. Stately home.

Dyserth Waterfall. C. Scenic attraction.

FFESTINIOG

GWYNEDD   **D4**

Ffestiniog is a neighbour of bigger and better-known Blaenau Ffestiniog. Both share the same robust appearance, a look dominated by rows of dark-stoned houses which are a more familiar sight in the valleys of South Wales than in the mountains of the north.

The village stands amongst powerful scenery, on the approach to the Migneint, an unexplored, boggy moorland wilderness. The scenery in the opposite direction is much more seductive. The village is perched on a high bluff overlooking the lovely Vale of Ffestiniog – one of Wales's classic beauty spots – a deep, sheltered valley of green rivermeadows and thick woodlands. There is a wealth of attractive scenery close by, including the Cynfal Falls, accessible by a footpath leading south from the village's old railway station. The rock above the falls, known as Huw Llwyd's Pulpit, is named after a 17th-century wizard, poet and sportsman. There are more waterfalls a few miles further up the river at Rhaeadr-y-cwm, visible from the B4391.

FLINT
CLWYD   **F2/3**   *i*

On first appearances, Flint may seem to hold little interest for the visitor. But look behind the run-of-the-mill main street and you will find a squat medieval castle, on land overlooking the Dee estuary. Flint Castle is historically significant as the first of the fortresses to be built by the English king, Edward 1, as part of his master plan to subdue the Welsh. Although a harbinger of mighty strongholds such as Caernarfon and Conwy, Flint, begun in 1277, is not in the same class as Edward's later castles.

The castle's relative obscurity can be explained by its location, bypassed by a through-route to the more popular parts of North Wales. Whilst it lacks the grandeur of Caernarfon, Flint Castle nevertheless merits closer attention. Its most upstanding remnant is its Great Tower which, like the rest of the castle, was surrounded by a moat. The stronghold makes an appearance in Shakespeare's *Richard 11* as the setting for the capture of the king by his rival, Henry Bolingbroke. Richard was taken from Flint to London, where he abdicated in favour of Bolingbroke, who became Henry 1V.

There is a Tourist Information Centre nearby on the A55 (Little Chef Services) at Halkyn.

Flint Castle. C. The first of Edward 1's 'iron ring' of Welsh castles. ✛

Nearby
Clover Casuals, The Old Church School, Halkyn. Tel (0352) 780666. F. Designer knitwear. Showrooms and workrooms just off A55 Expressway.

Flint Castle, the first of a new breed of fortresses

FRONCYSYLLTE
CLWYD   **F4**

Thomas Telford's engineering masterpiece, the Pontcysyllte Aqueduct, was built in 1805 to carry the Llangollen Canal across the river Dee. It can be approached from the village of Froncysyllte via the canal towpath. Nineteen arches support the structure. They are so tall and slim that Telford's critics doubted they could ever support their weight of water and masonry, let alone the canal traffic.

Canal boats carrying holidaymakers still sail regularly across the aqueduct. When viewed from a distance these craft deceptively appear as 'longboats flying in the sky'. For safety's sake, visitors who have no head for heights should not attempt to walk on its windy 307m (1006ft) iron gangway, which stands 39m (121ft) above the rushing waters of the Dee.

GLYNCEIRIOG
CLWYD   **F4**

Hidden deep in a narrow valley between the Berwyn mountains, Glynceiriog creates the feeling of a village forgotten by the world. It is the heart of Welsh Wales where a male-voice choir practises in a hall displaying mementos of three revered Welsh poets, all of them sons of the valley.

The Chwarel Wynne Slate Mine was once a village lifeline providing employment to men and boys. Today its caverns are busy in a different way as visitors arrive to view the mine's museum and to take guided tours through its eerie tunnels.

The valley's remote landscape, running for 16 miles beside the river Ceiriog, attracts pony trekkers, rough shooters, walkers and fishermen. Several comfortable hotels cater both for guests wanting to enjoy these activities, and for those who wish simply to absorb the valley's atmosphere of peace and rural tranquillity.

Ceiriog Institute. Tel (069172) 8910. F. Village hall. Museum-style display honours three local poets: Ceiriog (John Hughes); Eos Ceiriog (Huw Morris); and Cynddelw (Robert Ellis).

Chwarel Wynne Slate Mine and Museum. Tel (069172) 343. C. Floodlit displays, a museum and video theatre, illustrate life in a Victorian quarrying village.

GRESFORD
CLWYD   **F3**

Gresford's parish church rivals Wrexham's St Giles's in reputation and interest. It is judged to be of outstanding architectural merit and is famed for a brilliant collection of stained glass dating from medieval times. Its bells are listed amongst the so-called 'Seven Wonders' of Wales though a still greater wonder must be a yew tree in the churchyard rumoured to be over 1400 years old.

The rugged slopes above Holyhead are rich in historical remains

HAWARDEN

CLWYD   **F3**

Hawarden's image is that of a country village, despite its proximity to large centres of population. Because its site commands the Cheshire Plain, Hawarden has been fought over by warring armies since the days of William the Conqueror. The nearby Welsh stronghold, Ewloe Castle, was a battleground between Edward I and Llywelyn, Prince of Wales. Hawarden Castle, built by Edward, was not finally brought to ruins until the Civil War.

The town's rich historical tradition continued when, in 1852, the Prime Minister, W E Gladstone, married Catherine Glynne and set up residence locally in Broadlane Hall. In 1896, Gladstone founded a residential study centre in Hawarden before presenting the institution with his huge personal library. Today, the much-enlarged St Deiniol's Library, a splendid neo-Gothic building in extensive grounds, accommodates research students of all ages.

Several historic buildings enhance the town's character. They include St Deiniol's Ash Farm, an Elizabethan structure; St Deiniol's Church with its magnificent Gladstone family memorials; and the 'House of Correction', a 17th-century 'lock-up'.

Hawarden Old Castle. F. Remains of stone fortress dating from about 1280.

Nearby
Ewloe Castle (at southern end of Wepre Park – see Queensferry entry). F. Welsh native fortress with characteristic D-shaped tower. ✿

HOLYHEAD

GWYNEDD   **B2**

The port and holiday centre of Holyhead is truly at the 'end of the road' – the important cross-country A5 route. Next to the Custom House at the entrance to the harbour stands an arch – built to commemorate a visit by George 1V in 1821 – which looks like a miniature version of London's Marble Arch. The arch marks the official end of the A5, the 267-mile London to Holyhead route, much of which was pioneered by that great roadbuilder, Thomas Telford. In 1811, he surveyed a route from Shrewsbury to Holyhead through the difficult, mountainous terrain of Snowdonia. The final link in the A5's chain was completed when he built the ³/₄-mile-long Stanley Embankment which connects Holy island, on which Holyhead stands, to the rest of Anglesey.

The town still plays an important communications role as an Irish Sea ferry port. The harbour is protected by a Victorian breakwater – Britain's longest – which extends for more than a mile across Holyhead Bay from Soldiers' Point. Holyhead's long links with the sea are recalled at the town's Maritime Museum.

Holyhead has ancient roots. The Romans settled here, establishing a fort known as Caer Gybi, possibly as the base for a small naval flotilla. Its well-preserved rectangular walls enclose another ancient site, St Cybi's Church. This was founded in about AD550, though as it now stands it dates from the 13th century. Its airy interior contains a striking pre-Raphaelite window and figures together with the huge tomb of the Stanley family. A small reconstructed chapel in the churchyard housed the first free school to educate the poor children of Holyhead.

The influence of the Stanley family over local affairs dates from the time when Lord Stanley of Alderley married the heiress of Penrhos, an estate on the south-eastern approach to the town, in 1763. Most visitors arrive at Holyhead by crossing the Stanley Embankment, at the end of which is the entrance (by an old octagonal tollhouse built by Telford) to the Penrhos Coastal Park. There are beautiful coastal and woodland walks in the park, through a nature reserve and beside the calm waters of Beddmanarch Bay.

Holyhead is located on a little island scattered with a remarkable profusion of ancient sites. One of the oldest is the Trefignath Burial Chamber, of neolithic (New Stone Age) origin. Excavations here have revealed a long and complicated history. The burial place, originally a simple tomb and passage-way encased in a large cairn, was later enlarged to form a wedge-shaped mound which housed a second chamber.

The rugged slopes of Holyhead mountain contain the biggest concentration of sites. The Holyhead Mountain Hut Group consists of about 20 circular hut foundations and some smaller buildings. These are the only survivors of a much larger native farming settlement that existed here in Roman times, though this site was occupied before then – possibly in the late neolithic period.

Caer y Tŵr Hillfort stands at the 219m (720ft) summit of the mountain overlooking Holyhead Bay and the Irish Sea. Iron Age man built this strong-hold, though in later times the Romans added a watchtower – which may have been linked with Caer Gybi – probably as a look-out for Irish raiders. Other historic sites in this area include the mysteri-ous Bronze Age standing stones of Penrhos Feilw (on the minor road to Penrhosfeilw 1¼ miles south-west of Holyhead) and Tŷ Mawr (on the B4545 at the southern approach to the town).

Holyhead mountain drops down to the sea in a severe, spectacular fashion. South Stack, the westernmost tip of Holy island, is a rocky promon-tory jutting out into the waves and crowned by a lighthouse (no public access) which warns shipping off a curtain of sheer cliffs. South Stack's cliffs, which plunge more than 91m (300ft) to the sea, are made of some of the oldest rocks in the world. This part of the coast is famous for its sea-bird colonies as well as its scenery. To enjoy one of the best views, go to Ellin's Tower, a castellated Victorian building on the headland which is now a Royal Society for the Protection of Birds observatory (much of the headland is an RSPB reserve). Clear-day views from this stunning spot extend past the Llŷn peninsula as far as the Isle of Man and Ireland.

Caer Gybi Roman Fortlet. F. Walls still stand to a remarkable height in places. Dates from the 3rd century. ✠

Holyhead Leisure Centre. Tel (0407) 764111. C. Swimming pools, squash, sports hall.

Holyhead Maritime Museum. Tel (0407) 762816. C. Old photographs, models and other maritime artefacts tell the story of Holyhead and western Anglesey.

Nearby
Caer y Tŵr Hillfort (1¾ miles west of Holyhead – follow one of the footpaths to the summit of Holyhead mountain). F. Well laid-out, magnificently sited remains. Stone rampart still retains its sentry walk. ✠

Holyhead Mountain Hut Group (located off the minor road on the approach to South Stack, about 2½ miles west of Holyhead). F. Remnants of ancient mountain settlement. Original hearths and slab beds can still be seen within huts. ✠

Penrhos Coastal Park (off A5 at western end of Stanley Embankment). Tel (0407) 760949. F. 81-hectare (200-acre) park. Woodland and coastal walks, information centre, excellent viewing for waders and wildfowl in sheltered bay.

Trefignath Burial Chamber (on minor road 1 mile south-east of Holyhead). F. Walls, uprights and capstones of a prehistoric site built in different phases. ✠

HOLYWELL
CLWYD   F2

Holywell's fame derives from St Winefride's Well. The shrine which has existed as a place of healing and pilgrimage since the 7th century has become known as the 'Lourdes of Wales'. Legend has it that a spring rose from the ground where the severed head of an innocent young virgin fell after she was killed in anger by a prince whose advances she had rejected. St Beuno, Winefride's uncle, was present at the killing. He at once placed the head beside the body and prayed that she might be made whole again, whereupon Winefride rose to her feet, a white scar around her neck remaining as witness to her martyrdom.

Kings and queens have prayed at the well in the past and made rich gifts to it. Modern visitors can still expect to share this shrine with pilgrims who have faith in its healing powers. The stone by the

St Winefride's Well

Take a walk through the woods in the Greenfield valley

steps in the outer bath is reputed to be St Beuno's Stone, so called because this is where the saint sat to instruct Winefride.

The Greenfield Valley Heritage Park contains much of Holywell's agricultural and industrial past. The ruins of Basingwerk Abbey, home of Cistercian monks for 400 years, lie opposite historic Abbey Farm. A number of old farm buildings have been moved to this spot from the surrounding area and lovingly restored in the style of the period. The agricultural museum includes displays of rural crafts, and a film show in the Coleshill Barn traces the history of the valley. Along the line of an old railway, derelict cotton mills, copper works, and several reservoirs recall the valley's prosperous industrial past.

Basingwerk Abbey. F. Ruins of 12th-century abbey. ✠

Greenfield Valley Heritage Park. Museum tel (0352) 714172. Park F. Museum C. Find out all about Holywell's history.

Holywell Leisure Centre. Tel (0352) 712027. C. Large swimming pool, corkscrew waterslide and excellent sports facilities.

St Winefride's Well. Tel (0352) 713054. C. One of the traditional 'Seven Wonders of Wales'. ✠

LLANARMON DYFFRYN CEIRIOG
CLWYD   F4

One of Wales's best-loved poets was born here in 1832. John Hughes, known by his bardic name Ceiriog, wrote sentimental verses to some of the most poignant old Welsh melodies, including 'Dafydd y Garreg Wen' (David of the White Rock). His birthplace is a beautiful and isolated village in the Ceiriog valley, and his life is commemorated on a plaque in the unusual church, which has an austere design but two pulpits!

A 1000-year-old yew tree grows in the church-yard, which is laid out alongside the Ceiriog river. The village itself is well cared for, with flowers decorating the streets and houses.

LLANARMON YN IAL
CLWYD   F3

This delightful village nestles at the southern end of the Clwydian Range, a barrier of rounded hills above the Vale of Clwyd. Llanarmon's church, dedicated to St Germanus, has two naves separated by an 18th-century wooden arcade. Its shining treasure, though, is its three-tiered brass chandelier, an elaborate early 16th-century work of art.

The name *Yale* derives from Ial. The Yales, an important border family, had a manor house here. David Yale was one of the Pilgrim Fathers who sailed to America. His grandson, Elihu, played a key role in the founding of the famous American university (see Wrexham entry).

LLANBEDROG
GWYNEDD   B4

A headland shelters Llanbedrog's popular sands

Llanbedrog's main appeal is as a beach resort, for its sheltered sands are particularly attractive to families. Canoes and boats can be hired here, and there are several wooded walks nearby. A rocky outcrop known as Mynydd Tir y Cwmwd looks out over Tremadog Bay and is now guarded by a lone figure called the Tin Man. This life-size statue has been watching the horizon since 1980, when it was erected to take the place of an old landmark. The original 'man of the mountain' was a 2m- (8ft-) high figurehead, brought from a Cardiff sailing ship in 1919 by the Andrews family, owners of the neo-Gothic mansion Plas Glyn-y-Weddw. Having been a familiar and much-photographed sight for 60 years, the 'old man' was eventually pulled down after being vandalized. A good view of his substitute can be had from Glyn-y-Weddw, which now houses a gallery of Welsh art and temporary exhibitions.

The simple parish church, on the road which leads to the beach, is dedicated to St Pedrog, a 6th-century preacher who travelled in Wales, Devon, Cornwall and Brittany. The building was restored in the 19th century but its screen and font are 16th century, and the west window has pieces of glass from an earlier, medieval window, said to have been broken by Oliver Cromwell's soldiers. Maintenance of the church was paid for in the past by the Love-Parry family, whose name appears in several of its memorials. This Puritan family first settled here in the 17th century and it was one of its descendants, Lady Love-Jones-Parry, who built Plas Glyn-y-Weddw.

Plas Glyn-y-Weddw Historic House and Art Gallery. Tel (0758) 740763. C. Displays of Welsh art in beautifully furnished mansion on a hill overlooking the bay.

Lakeside Llanberis stands at the approach to the highest mountains in England and Wales

LLANBERIS

GWYNEDD   C3

Llanberis attracts serious climbers, weekend walkers and visitors who are content to enjoy its lakeside setting at the foot of Snowdon, at 1085m (3560ft) the highest peak in Britain south of the Scottish Highlands. The one road that everyone inevitably wants to drive along is the Llanberis pass, which claws its way up from the town past sheer rock slabs and slopes littered with huge boulders to Pen-y-Pass, a popular starting point for two paths to the summit of Snowdon.

The gentlest – if not the shortest – of the paths to the summit starts at Llanberis itself, though the easiest way to get to the top is by the famous Snowdon Mountain Railway. This narrow-gauge line, the only public rack-and-pinion railway in Britain, chuffs its way laboriously for over 4½ miles to an upper terminus just short of the summit – keep an eye on the weather and choose a clear day if you want to enjoy one of the most breathtaking views in Britain, extending as far as Ireland's Wicklow hills. Those without a head for heights might prefer the Llanberis Lake Railway, another delightful narrow-gauge line, which follows a 2½-mile route along Llyn Padarn.

Llanberis has grown up beside two lakes, Llyn Peris and Llyn Padarn. The slopes above the lakes bear witness to intensive quarrying activity. In its heyday, the Dinorwig Slate Quarry was one of Wales's largest, employing over 3000 men. Following its closure in 1969, the workshops were preserved as the Welsh Slate Museum. Everything remains as it was – the machinery, plant and huge waterwheel, over 15m (50ft) in diameter, which once powered the workshops – when the quarry supplied the world with roofing slates.

(contd overleaf)

Take a train ride to the top on the Snowdon Mountain Railway

Welsh Slate Museum

The slate rubble and massive staircase of terraces carved into the face of the mountain above Llyn Peris, the result of intensive 19th-century industrial activity, have an invisible late 20th-century equivalent. The inside of the mountain has been hewn out to accommodate an awesome system of gigantic chambers and tunnels over 10 miles long in the construction of the Dinorwig hydro-electric pumped-storage scheme. The chamber housing the main plant is one of the largest man-made caverns ever created – twice as long as a football pitch and higher than a 16-storey building.

The principle behind the scheme sounds deceptively simple. Water, pumped up from the lake to a reservoir at the top of the mountain, then rushes down through the heart of the mountain to power turbines which create huge amounts of electricity for the National Grid. The engineering achievements in creating such a scheme have to be seen to be believed – a visit to the Power of Wales museum includes an unforgettable trip into this fantastic, futuristic underground world.

The Padarn Country Park is based around the shores of Llyn Padarn. The land, once part of the huge Dinorwig Slate Quarry, includes a hillside of oak woodlands and a network of walks, one of which leads to the former Quarry Hospital which contains wildlife exhibits and displays of original medical equipment. The lake is a busy watersports centre popular with sailors, canoeists and windsurfers. Another of the many attractive walks in and around Llanberis leads to Ceunant Mawr, an impressive waterfall above the town.

The narrow strip of land separating the two lakes was the obvious place to site the stronghold of Dolbadarn Castle, which guards the northern entrance to the Llanberis pass. This robust, single-towered castle was built by the medieval Welsh leader Llywelyn the Great.

Dolbadarn Castle. C. Tall round keep dating from early 13th century. In dramatic location overlooking lakes. ✦

Llanberis Lake Railway. Tel (0286) 870549. C. Runs along the scenic shores of Llyn Padarn for 2 miles.

Padarn Country Park. Tel (0286) 870892. F. Lakeside setting which combines natural beauty with industrial heritage. Information kiosk, walks, craft workshops, picnic areas. Llanberis Lake Railway and Welsh Slate Museum located within park.

Piggery Pottery. Tel (0286) 872529. F. Large lakeside pottery. Throw or paint your own pot (C).

Power of Wales – Museum of the North. Tel (0286) 870636. C. Wales's history presented in a novel, imaginative way. Natural science theatre, multi-media programme on electricity. Don't miss the highlight – an underground tour of the largest pumped-storage power station in Europe. ✦

Snowdon Mountain Railway. Tel (0286) 870223. C. Climbs over 900m (2953ft) almost to Snowdon's summit. Must be the most spectacular train ride in Britain.

Welsh Slate Museum. Tel (0286) 870630. C. Original workshops, machinery and plant. Displays and demonstrations of the quarryman's work. ✦

Nearby
Bryn Brâs Castle, Llanrug. Tel (0286) 870210. C. Castellated Welsh mansion built in about 1830. Comfortable, stylish interiors, splendid gardens and grounds covering 13 hectares (32 acres).

LLANDDEUSANT

GWYNEDD   B2

Travelling around the Isle of Anglesey, you'll see the occasional ruined windmill. Days gone by, the island – known historically as 'the granary of Wales' – supported over 50 working windmills.

The peaceful village of Llanddeusant contains the only working mill left on the island. You won't have any trouble finding it. Llynnon Mill stands on a slight rise in flat farming country on the outskirts of the village. It was built in the 1770s and worked until 1918, when it suffered severe storm damage. The mill has now been restored to full health. Visitors can climb steep stairs and see the four levels of the mill, following the milling sequences from top to bottom as the grain is processed into flour. The old grain store opposite contains an exhibition which records the mill's restoration.

Llynnon Mill. Tel (0407) 730797/730687. C. The only working windmill in Wales.

LLANDRILLO

CLWYD   E4

Llandrillo stands in the undisturbed Vale of Edeyrnion between Bala and Corwen. The fertile farmlands of the vale contrast with the exposed, open moorlands of the Berwyn mountains rising to the east. Walkers can set off from the village for the heights of Cadair Bronwen and Cadair Berwyn, about 3¹/₂ miles to the south-east.

A LOOK AT WELSH HISTORY

Bryn Celli Ddu Burial Chamber

Valle Crucis Abbey

Caernarfon Castle

Wales's reputation as a land of castles springs from the medieval fortresses of the north. The 'iron ring' of 13th-century castles built by the English king Edward 1 to contain the Welsh survive as reminders of a troubled age. Their power and presence remain undimmed even to this day. Caernarfon, Wales's most famous castle, retains the aura of a royal palace as well as that of a military stronghold. And Conwy's soaring, dark-stoned defences, complemented by a ring of walls which still encircles the old town, continue to evoke a chillingly authentic medieval spirit.

The wealth of historic monuments in these parts is unparalleled. Beaumaris, Rhuddlan, Denbigh and Flint all have at their core medieval strongholds built as part of a master plan to conquer the Welsh. The other side to the coin can be seen at places such as Llanberis and Dolwyddelan, where the Welsh princes built their mountain strongholds.

These castles are newcomers when judged by the timescales that apply to the many prehistoric sites on the Isle of Anglesey. Ancient tombs such as Bryn Celli Ddu and Barclodiad y Gawres permit a fleeting glimpse into a dim, distant and ultimately mysterious past.

Welsh history's more peaceful, contemplative side is represented by the ruins of Valle Crucis Abbey, a Cistercian monastery near Llangollen, and St Winefride's Well, a long-established place of pilgrimage and one of the traditional 'Seven Wonders of Wales'.

The forces of change are charted in bricks and mortar at Chirk Castle, a sumptuous stately home that evolved over the centuries from a simple border fortress. Chirk, along with the mansions of Erddig, Plas Newydd (on Anglesey) and Penrhyn Castle, are monuments to a privileged style of life. Penrhyn, near Bangor, is a product of the relatively recent past. The 'castle' was built as a grand house in the 19th century with the wealth created by North Wales's slate industry. In stark contrast, the underground world of the slate miner can be seen in caverns at Blaenau Ffestiniog open to the public, while Llanberis, another old slate-mining community, has preserved its quarry workshops.

Handsome Plas Newydd, near Llanfair PG

Llandudno lies neatly between two headlands

Travellers who need to revive their confidence in the British seaside should go to Llandudno. It's a place which personifies the perfect vision of the seaside resort untainted by the garishness which despoils parts of the British coast. Llandudno is redolent of order, sympathetic planning, space, harmony and an altogether more genteel age. The seafront is lined with a wide promenade backed by row after row of elegant Victorian façades painted in dazzling colours, the entire scene perfectly framed by the cliffs of the Great and Little Orme headlands.

Llandudno has two fine beaches. At the North Shore children can swim in safety, ride a donkey, enjoy Punch and Judy, play in the paddling pool, sail model yachts, romp in the playground, or build sandcastles in the shadow of Llandudno's magnificent pier where optimistic fishermen hang out their lines. The second beach, at the lovely West Shore, is popular with yachtsmen and windsurfers.

The Great Orme rears 207m (679ft) out of the sea. There are innumerable places of interest to explore hidden among the cliffs and pathways of this towering limestone hump, which stands guard over the town's western approaches like a miniature Rock of Gibraltar. The old Norse word *orme* means 'sea monster', a description easily understood when mists shroud the cliffs and play tricks with the eyes.

Llandudno's history is closely linked to the story of the copper mines which once thrived on the Orme. The mines, dating from the Bronze Age, have recently been reopened to visitors. It's now possible to walk underground through ancient workings and see the conditions under which prehistoric man mined for copper.

A dramatic, but short-lived, expansion in mining activity took place during the 1830s. When mining activity collapsed in the 1840s Llandudno began to carve a new career for itself as a Victorian resort. This development was encouraged by improved road and rail communications from the prosperous industrial centres of Manchester and Liverpool, and the new Victorian craze for sea bathing. The master plan for the town's conversion into a classic Victorian resort was initiated and controlled by the Mostyn family, whose influence as landowners was so great that it assured strict control of any development. The resort's unique charm comes from the way in which it has preserved its original character. The Llandudno of today is not that different from the Llandudno of yesterday.

The popular Marine Drive which is carved into the face of the Great Orme runs for miles beside stunning vistas of land and sea. Paths, steep in parts,

Ski Llandudno allows you to ski at a seaside resort

38

lead to the Orme's summit, though the ascent can be made effortlessly on one of Llandudno's San Franciscan-style passenger trams, or alpine-style by cable car. All ascents end in spectacular views of the coast and mountains of Snowdonia which lie tantalizingly close across the Conwy estuary.

Once at the summit children can have fun in an adventure playground. Birdwatching in the Great Orme Country Park is popular; so too is the urge to spot the Orme's resident herd of wild Kashmir goats. The Orme's visitor centre contains displays on the headland's geological and historical importance, including the story of of its once-famous copper mines. Head next for St Tudno's, a restored 12th-century church. St Tudno brought Christianity to this area in the 6th century at a time when the coast was under constant threat from marauders. The original church was probably built in this commanding site above the sea because of its defensive qualities. Open-air services are occasionally held here in summer.

Lower down the Orme is Ski Llandudno, where you'll find one of the longest artificial ski slopes in Britain, nursery slopes and a 213m (700ft) toboggan run. Close by are the delightful semi-tropical gardens of Happy Valley which lie in the shadow of the Orme.

As a shopping centre Llandudno has no rival in North Wales. In streets such as Lloyd Street, where handsome 19th-century cast iron arcades still shelter the shopfronts, shoppers take pleasure in the atmosphere of a grander age.

The variety of things to see and do means no one needs feel deprived, even on a rainy day. On Mostyn Broadway a heated indoor swimming pool ensures that everyone can enjoy a daily swim; the Mostyn Art Gallery in Vaughan Street presents a variety of exhibitions throughout the year whilst actively promoting Welsh culture; and the Childhood Revisited attraction, Bodhyfryd Road, contains an outstanding collection of dolls, a model railway and British motorcycles dating from 1914.

Children also flock to The Rabbit Hole in Trinity Square, where an Alice in Wonderland grotto features an exhibition of Alice's adventures. Alice Pleasance Liddell, immortalized by Lewis Carroll as 'Alice', holidayed in Llandudno as a child. The resort's association with the story is reflected in a memorial to the White Rabbit, unveiled on the West Shore in 1933.

Llandudno's excellent outdoor activities include golf (at four 18-hole courses), bowls, tennis, pony trekking, horse riding, sailing, fishing and pitch and putt. At the huge indoor Canolfan Aberconwy Centre on the promenade visitors can play badminton, squash, carpet bowls and other sports. This versatile centre, which incorporates the Arcadia Theatre, is also a venue for big-name summer shows, orchestral concerts, dancing, discos, cabaret and performances by Welsh choirs and brass bands. Throughout the resort many leading hotels, their façades ablaze with light, allow non-residents to attend their evening entertainment programmes.

Visit the magical world of Alice in Wonderland

Alice In Wonderland Visitor Centre, The Rabbit Hole, 3/4 Trinity Square. Tel (0492) 860082. C. A must for Lewis Carroll fans.

Cabin Lift, Happy Valley. Tel (0492) 877205. C. Float from Happy Valley Station to the Great Orme summit by cable car.

Canolfan Aberconwy Centre/Arcadia Theatre, The Promenade. Tel (0492) 879771. C. Leisure centre and theatre complex. Entertainment and sporting facilities.

Childhood Revisited, Bodhyfryd Road. Tel (0492) 870424. C. Dolls, model railway and motorcycles.

Great Orme Country Park Information Centre (at the summit). Tel (0492) 874151. F. Displays explain geology, history and natural history of the Orme since prehistoric times.

Great Orme Mines. Tel (0492) 870477. C. See how copper was mined in ancient times. Underground visit, audio-visual display. No parking at mine. Access by free shuttle bus or Great Orme Tramway.

Great Orme Tramway, Victoria Station, Church Walks. Tel (0492) 870870. C. Ride by tram to the summit of the Great Orme. Joint ticket which includes admission to Great Orme Mines available.

Mostyn Art Gallery, 12 Vaughan Street. Tel (0492) 874151. F. Exhibitions. Welsh culture.

Ski Llandudno, Great Orme. Tel (0492) 874707. C. Ski and toboggan without snow.

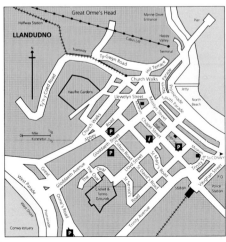

LLANFAIRFECHAN

GWYNEDD   C3

Llanfairfechan is laid out along a narrow coastal strip backed by steep-sided mountains. It plays the role of the smaller seaside resort very well, and is popular with those who wish to avoid the hurly-burly of the bigger, more commercial places along the North Wales coast. The low-tide sands are wide and firm, there is a promenade, the streets have a pleasant Victorian character, and the resort, although small, boasts a good range of facilities.

This is an ideal spot for those wishing to combine hill walking with a seaside holiday. The uplands behind the resort can be explored by following a number of trails, one of which runs along sections of an old Roman road which linked bases at Chester and Caernarfon. Another popular local walk leads from Bont Newydd (off the main road at Aber, 2 miles to the south-west) to the beautiful Aber Falls.

LLANFAIR PG

GWYNEDD   C3

Try to pronounce the world's longest placename

No self-respecting guidebook to North Wales could possibly avoid having to spell Llanfair PG's tongue-twisting, world-beating placename in full, so here goes: Llanfairpwllgwyngyllgogerychwyrndrobwll-llantysiliogogogoch, which means 'St Mary's (Church) by the white aspen over the whirlpool, and St Tysilio's (Church) by the red cave'. Locals have understandably grown tired of pronouncing, in full, the world's longest placename, shortening it to a more manageable Llanfair PG or Llanfairpwll. It seems churlish to have to point out that the quirky name was created in the 19th century by a local tradesman to publicize the place.

The name is displayed in its full glory on shopfronts and at the impressive James Pringle complex, an attractively designed building on the railway station site which contains a huge selection of woollens and craft items. Llanfair PG stands on the original A5 (the village is now bypassed), the

road built by Thomas Telford to transform communications between England, North Wales and the port of Holyhead. An octagonal Holyhead Road tollhouse, complete with list of tolls, can be seen at the entrance to the village. Llanfair PG was the birthplace of the British Women's Institute movement, an idea imported from Canada in 1915.

The Marquess of Anglesey's Column, undoubtedly the best viewpoint on the Isle of Anglesey, stands on the eastern outskirts of Llanfair PG. The column was erected in 1816 to commemorate the military achievements of the marquess, who served as Wellington's second-in-command at the 1815 Battle of Waterloo, at which he lost a leg. A spiral wooden staircase of 115 steps leads to a lofty platform from which there are tremendous views of the Britannia Bridge (see Menai Bridge entry), the Menai Strait, Snowdonia and Anglesey's flatlands. The marquess's sumptuous home, Plas Newydd, is in the care of the National Trust and open to the public.

The nearby village of Penmynydd was the home of the early Tudors, ancestors of Harri Tudur who, when he became Henry V11 in 1485, founded the all-powerful Tudor dynasty of monarchs. References to this historic family are contained in the local church.

James Pringle. Tel (0248) 717171. F. Huge selection of quality woollen and craft products.

Marquess of Anglesey's Column. Tel (0248) 714393. C. 27m (90ft) column built on wooded hillock.

Nearby
Bryn Celli Ddu Burial Chamber (in field off minor road 1¹/₂ miles south-west of village). F. About ¹/₂-mile walk from road. Unlike many prehistoric tombs, Bryn Celli Ddu resembles its original appearance since its stone frame is covered by an earthen mound. Take a torch. ✪

Plas Newydd (2 miles south-west of village off A4080). Tel (0248) 714795. C. Elegant 18th-century mansion located in lovely grounds on banks of Menai Strait. Military Museum displays campaign relics of 1st marquess, including his famous wooden leg. Rex Whistler Exhibition's centrepiece is the artist's largest wall painting, a stunning work. Beautiful rooms and gardens. 🌿

LLANGEFNI

GWYNEDD   C2

Llangefni's central location on the Isle of Anglesey makes it a natural meeting place. The focal point of this busy crossroads town, shopping and administrative centre is a grey-stoned clock tower (of 1902) and sturdy market hall. Not surprisingly, Llangefni is the island's main marketplace – a large open-air market is held every Thursday. There are pleasant walks in The Dingle, a wooded valley leading north-west from the town in the direction of the Cefni reservoir, whose waters attract migrant wildfowl and fishermen.

Wildlife artist Charles Tunnicliffe spent much of his life in these parts (see Aberffraw entry). A collection of his paintings, together with works by other artists – including Kyffin Williams – can be seen in the new art gallery on the fringes of town.

Oriel Ynys Môn, Rhosmeirch. Tel (0248) 724444. C. Art gallery, historic displays, temporary exhibitions.

Plas Arthur Leisure Centre. Tel (0248) 722966. C. Swimming pools, sports hall, climbing wall, squash, tennis and bowls.

Nearby
Bodeilio Craft Centre, Talwrn. Tel (0248) 722535. F. Knitwear centre – see small-scale knitting industry at work. Mill shop.

Hen Blas Country Park (off B4422 about 3 miles south-west of Llangefni). Tel (0407) 840152. C. 93-hectare (230-acre) park with lots to see and do including 17th-century manor house, gardens, shire horses, falconry and craft displays, wildlife room, audio-visual theatre. Boasts the largest indoor play area in North Wales.

Stone Science (on B5109 about 3 miles north-east of Llangefni). Tel (0248) 70310. C. Fossils, minerals, rocks and crystals from all over the world. Collection includes spearheads and petrified dinosaur bones. Slide show on geology of Anglesey.

Hen Blas Country Park

LLANGOLLEN

CLWYD   F4

Approach Llangollen from the east and you get the feeling, abruptly and unmistakably, that you are in Wales. Your route, through the wide, flattish borderlands, suddenly funnels into a narrow, steep-sided valley. Mountains, rocky escarpments and forests encircle the town, a ruined fortress stands guard above it and a rushing river divides it. The contrast between open border country and looming mountains is made even more acute by the fact that Llangollen is only a few miles within Wales.

The town has developed gracefully beside the banks of the river Dee. This characteristic is easily observed on a Town Trail walk (details at the Tourist Information Centre), during which Llangollen's narrow streets reveal the half-timbered façade of an ancient hide and skin tannery, the Gothic towers of a famous hotel and simple period cottages sandwiched between stylish Georgian and Victorian frontages.

Llangollen, on the banks of the Dee

At the town centre a 14th-century bridge presides over the Dee, a river renowned for its fishing. The north bank is home to the Llangollen Railway Society which has restored the station yard and several miles of track into a successful working standard-gauge steam railway. Excursions up the Dee valley attract enthusiasts from far and wide. In winter the swollen floodwaters of the Dee attract canoeists prepared to bob and tumble in the river's wild white waters.

In contrast, nothing disturbs the waters of the Llangollen Canal except the passage of horse-drawn boats wafting passengers up the valley to the famous Horseshoe Falls. Exhibits in a Canal Museum tell the story of Britain's inland waterways. Idyllic towpath walks reach out for miles to the east and west from the museum wharf along a canal, described by a canal-boat chronicler as 'the most beautiful waterway in the country'.

Close to the museum a path leads to the hilltop above Llangollen occupied by the stumpy ruins of Castell Dinas Brân. The 12th-century fortress was built by the Prince of Powys as a base from which to raid the English borders. It is a stiff, though popular, walk up to the hoary old ruin.

A public park and picnic area are located on the riverbank facing the railway station. Young children love this spot where hundreds of greedy ducks gather in rocky pools to be fed. Below the weir, in an old woollen mill, you'll find an exact replica of a Victorian schoolroom.

A tastefully restored Welsh chapel on Castle Street is the base for the European Centre for Traditional and Regional Cultures. Llangollen hosts this prestigious institution because of its promotion of the International Musical Eisteddfod, a colourful, cosmopolitan festival of music and dancing, attracting participants from all over the world, which is held annually in July.

Plas Newydd, a half-timbered house in Tudor style, is Llangollen's most distinguished building and was the 18th-century home of the legendary 'Ladies of Llangollen'. Here lived Lady Eleanor Butler and Miss Sarah Ponsonby, two Irish women who eloped

41

together from Waterford. The Duke of Wellington and Sir Walter Scott were just two of the rich and famous who flocked to Llangollen to meet this unusual pair.

The Horseshoe pass, one of Wales's most famous beauty spots, lies 2 miles north of Llangollen on the A542. Though the drive to the summit above steep precipices can be unnerving, the spectacular views offered by vantage points *en route* make the journey unforgettable. In contrast, the majestic ruins of Valle Crucis Abbey stand at the foot of the pass amidst a scene of pastoral tranquillity. Its Abbot, Robert of Salisbury, was convicted in 1542 for highway robbery and minting counterfeit coins. Not far from the abbey look for the remains of Eliseg's Pillar, a sad monument to the memory of the pre-medieval kings of Powys.

Below Valle Crucis the road branches west on the A358 to the Velvet hill, thus named because in certain light conditions its slopes undergo a transformation to the colour of rich brown velvet. The famous Panorama rocks lie 1 mile east of Llangollen. Turn off the A358 by Sun Trevor Inn and follow a rock-strewn road to the top where the path winds round the flanks of the mountain 300m (about 1000ft) above the Vale of Llangollen. Other walkers may prefer a narrow valley mysteriously named World's End. A well-preserved Elizabethan hunting lodge emphasizes the valley's timeless atmosphere.

Canal Museum. Tel (0978) 860702. C. Inland waterway displays.

Castell Dinas Brân. F. Dominates the Dee valley and the town 'like a Rhineland castle mysteriously transported to Wales'.

Castell Dinas Brân, on its lofty perch above Llangollen

European Centre for Traditional and Regional Cultures (ECTARC). Tel (0978) 861292. F. Regular international exhibitions and concerts.

Llangollen Craft Centre. Tel (0978) 861887. C. Range of individual craft workshops in converted malthouse.

Llangollen Railway. Tel (0978) 860951. C. Steam trains, station and workshops.

Plas Newydd. Tel (0978) 861514. C. Attractive home of the 'Ladies of Llangollen'. Contains a fine collection of medieval oak carvings.

Victorian Schoolroom. Tel (0978) 860794. C. Complete with teacher's cane.

Nearby
Eliseg's Pillar (2 miles north on A542). F. 9th-century cross.

Motor Museum (1 mile west on A542). Tel (0978) 860324. C. Displays vehicles over 25 years old.

Valle Crucis Abbey (2 miles north on A542). Tel (0978) 860326. C. Ruined Cistercian abbey.

LLANGYBI
GWYNEDD   B4

The village is named after St Cybi, a 6th-century saint and healer of the sick who travelled widely in Wales. Ffynnon Gybi, or St Cybi's Well, is well worth seeking out. It stands in fields behind the village church, forgotten yet still charged with that special siren quality that once drew people to its healing waters. A mossy path leads to the well chamber, enclosed by rough stone walls which are part of a ruined cottage, a leftover from the 18th century when the well became a spa.

LLANRHAEADR YM MOCHNANT
CLWYD/POWYS   E4

Two counties meet here, marking the division between Mid and North Wales. With its intimate atmosphere and low stone cottages which follow the contours of the valley, Llanrhaeadr is a typically Welsh village with a predominantly Welsh-speaking community. It was here that Bishop William Morgan translated the Bible into Welsh in 1588 – an achievement which made a major contribution to the survival of the language – while he was vicar of the parish. A plaque on the church wall commemorates his association with the area.

A 4-mile road lined with rowan trees leads to the rhaeadr (waterfall) of the village name. Pistyll Rhaeadr, one of the traditional 'Seven Wonders of Wales', is a breathtaking sight, plunging 73m (240ft) in two stages over a sheer cliff, and passing under a 'fairy bridge' – a natural arch of rock – on its way down. At the foot of the waterfall is the pleasant Tan y Pistyll (Under the Spout) tea room, and a footpath leads into the hills, where you can gaze across the Rhaeadr valley to the peaks of the Berwyn mountains.

Pistyll Rhaeadr

It takes a lively imagination to visualize the castle which once stood among wooded hills near Llangedwyn, on the B4396 east of Llanrhaeadr ym Mochnant. An overgrown mound and low earthworks now form part of the surrounding pastureland, but on this spot Owain Glyndŵr, the 14th-/15th-century Welsh leader, once held court. This was Sycharth, immortalized in Welsh verse and folklore as the romantic focal point for the medieval independence movement.

LLANRWST
GWYNEDD   D3

Llanrwst's famous stone bridge over the Conwy

This attractive little market town, the 'capital of the Conwy valley', stands in a broad, luxuriant vale on the edge of thick forest and high mountain. Llanrwst's most famous feature is its old three-arched bridge across the Conwy, a river known since Roman times for its exquisite oyster pearls. The venerable stone structure is known in local tradition as Pont y Perl (The Bridge of the Pearl) because, at the laying of the foundation stone in 1636, a beautiful pearl was found. The bridge, believed to be the work of Inigo Jones, faces a riverside park with children's playground and other recreational facilities. The park's Gorsedd Circle of standing stones commemorates the holding of the National Eisteddfod at Llanrwst in 1951.

The old building at one end of the bridge is Tu Hwnt i'r Bont, a restored 15th-century house (once a courthouse) now owned by the National Trust and used as a tearoom.

Since Tudor times Llanrwst's development has been strongly influenced by the Wynn family of Gwydir Castle. Their house is a delightful example of a medieval dwelling, constructed in the style of fortress. The Wynns built Gwydir Chapel on to St Grwst's parish church in the 17th century. The chapel contains many treasures including a weighty stone coffin said to be that of Llywelyn ab Iorwerth, Llywelyn the Great, Prince of Gwynedd. Equally precious in the body of the church is a magnificently carved rood screen taken from Maenan Abbey, whose scant ruins lie north of the town.

There is another chapel, Gwydir Uchaf, in the woods above the town. Also built by the Wynns in the 17th century, it contains ceiling paintings of striking originality which have attracted the interest of art experts everywhere.

Llanrwst is an excellent walking and touring centre. Paths lead westwards into the woods and hills, where a series of little-visited lakes is hidden, two of which – Llyn Geirionydd and Llyn Crafnant – are particularly attractive.

Gwydir Uchaf Chapel (on forested slopes west of the river off B5106). Tel (0492) 640978. C. Fine carvings and painted ceiling. 🔵

LLANSANTFFRAID GLAN CONWY
GWYNEDD   D2

The village, which stands on the east bank of the river Conwy a short distance from Conwy, Llandudno and Colwyn Bay, is best known for the picturesque Felin Isaf Watermill. Though it is no longer in use, simple displays along a mill trail

Beautiful Bodnant Garden in the Vale of Conwy

clearly explain the watermill's history and workings. The dripping waterwheel, mysterious cogs and pulleys and the astonishing oat kiln contribute to a memorable visit.

Just a mile away is the famous Bodnant Garden, one of the finest gardens in Britain, overlooking the river Conwy and Snowdonia. Covering nearly 40 hectares (100 acres), it is full of colourful flowers, exotic shrubs and magnificent trees.

Felin Isaf Watermill. Tel (0492) 580646. C. 17th-century mill mostly in its original condition.

Nearby
Bodnant Garden (1 mile south on A470). Tel (0492) 650460. C. A garden for all seasons, especially early summer when rhododendrons and azaleas bloom, and the Laburnum Arch attains its full golden glory.
❧

One of the Urdd's permanent camps, Glanllyn, is based by Bala Lake in a mansion which was once home to the Williams-Wynns, who in the 19th century were the greatest landed family in Wales. This politically and territorially powerful family is recalled in an inscription on Llanuwchllyn's village pump, marking the birth of the heir to the Ruabon seat, Wynnstay, and in a plaque on a whitewashed cottage nearby.

At the Bala Lake Railway terminus, south of the village, you can watch the locomotive being prepared for its journey along a lovely lakeside route to Bala. A single trip along the lake's shore takes 25 minutes and can be broken at any of the four stations on the way for swimming, fishing, picnicking or walking.

Bala Lake Railway. Tel (06784) 666. C. Scenic trips on a narrow-gauge track along the shore of Bala Lake.

LLANUWCHLLYN

GWYNEDD   D4

Llanuwchllyn and Bala sit at either end of the 4-mile-long Llyn Tegid (Bala Lake), linked by the narrow-gauge Bala Lake Railway. Two of Llanuwchllyn's sons did much to ensure the survival of the Welsh language in the late 19th and 20th centuries. Owen Edwards, historian and scholar, promoted the use of Welsh literature in schools and was himself an author of many children's books. His son Ifan ab Owen Edwards, founded a lasting Welsh institution: Urdd Gobaith Cymru, the Welsh League of Youth, a movement which uses educational courses, outdoor activities and its own national eisteddfod to encourage the use of Welsh by children and teenagers. A statue of the two men stands at the northern end of Llanuwchllyn, and a strikingly designed gate has been erected outside the church in memory of Owen Edwards.

Helping hands at the Bala Lake Railway

LLANYSTUMDWY

GWYNEDD   C4

One of Britain's best-known statesmen grew up in this peaceful village straddling the river Dwyfor, 1½ miles west of Criccieth. David Lloyd George was a Liberal politician known for his powers of oratory, and responsible, as Chancellor of the Exchequer, for the introduction of National Health Insurance. After serving as Minister of Munitions and Minister of War in 1915–16, he became Prime Minister until his defeat in the General Election of 1922. Originally from Manchester, Lloyd George came to live in his widowed mother's home at an early age.

Not surprisingly, Lloyd George's name and influence dominate this little village. The cottage where he grew up, Highgate, still stands and is open to the public. A map outside the Post Office pinpoints the sites associated with the 'Welsh Wizard'. They include a half-timbered village institute, which he paid for after a successful libel action in 1909, and Tŷ Newydd (New House), the renovated building which became his last home. A museum dedicated to the life and times of this influential politician was extended to celebrate the centenary of his election to parliament in 1890; its features include an audio-visual theatre and Victorian schoolroom. Highgate Cottage has been furnished to recreate the period of Lloyd George's boyhood.

On the banks of the Dwyfor, a boulder where Lloyd George used to sit now marks his grave in an oval stone enclosure with a wrought-iron gate and the initials D Ll G set into the porch. The memorial gates opposite were a gift from Pwllheli in 1952, and carry the elephant and castle which figure in the town's coat of arms.

Dwyfor Ranch Rabbit Farm (above village). Tel (0766) 523136. C. Farm park with about 1000 rabbits and other animals.

Lloyd George Memorial Museum and Highgate Cottage. Tel (0286) 672255. C. Original furniture recalls Lloyd George's youth in Llanystumdwy and exhibition traces his political progress.

MYTHS AND LEGENDS

The Celts were great storytellers. Tales of heroism, romance, treachery and magic were passed on word-of-mouth and told in the courts of the Welsh princes. Many of these stories appear in the 'Mabinogion', Wales's first written collection of folk tales.

Truth or fiction? Read Gelert's legend for yourself at Beddgelert

North Wales's dramatic mountains and seashores must have provided a powerful stimulus to the imaginations of those early storytellers. The 'Mabinogion's' evocative Dream of Macsen Wledig describes Macsen's approach to Caernarfon from Snowdon, 'a harsh rugged terrain whose like he had never seen . . . (and) a great castle, the fairest that mortal had ever seen'.

For once, fiction may well be based on fact, for Macsen was Magnus Maximus, the Roman emperor who reputedly travelled to his fort of Segontium at Caernarfon. This is not to say that the Welsh are short of embellishment when it comes to adding a dash of local colour to stories. One of North Wales's tallest – and best known – tales involves the poignant death of the faithful hound Gelert (see Beddgelert entry). Like all good stories, it has a ring of truth, even though it was the work of a local innkeeper keen to draw attention to the village. Before we become too critical of the enterprising landlord, we should remember that folk tales are essentially based on inventiveness and entertainment.

The Isle of Anglesey, once a centre for the Druids, has a rich fund of supernatural tales involving ships that fly, hooded monks, sea-witches and haunting 'White Ladies', one of whom apparently appeared during the construction of the Wylfa Nuclear Power Station in the 1960s.

Inevitably, King Arthur also makes an appearance in these parts. There are caves where the slumbering saviour and his knights rest, awaiting the call once again to defend their land. In the centre of Ruthin is Maen Huail (Huail's Stone) where Arthur is said to have beheaded a rival.

Today's travellers can still see why North Wales was such a fertile breeding ground for folk tales. Go to some of its wilder parts – Snowdonia's rocky defiles or Llŷn's plunging cliffs – and experience for yourself those raw, elemental forces which find their way into so many stories.

North Wales's dramatic landscapes have inspired many a folk tale

LLITHFAEN
GWYNEDD B4

The rocky mass of Yr Eifl, a three-peaked mountain mass, looms above the village of Llithfaen. Yr Eifl (corrupted in English to The Rivals), rises to 564m (1850ft), the highest point on the Llŷn peninsula. These bleak, inhospitable but eminently defendable heights were chosen as the site of a native village, occupied in Roman times but of earlier origin, known as Tre'r Ceiri (The Town of the Giants). If you take the trouble to clamber up the mountain (follow the path off the B4417), you will see remarkable remains of a large stone village, including ramparts, gateways and the ruins of about 150 circular huts. You will also be rewarded with magnificent views of Llŷn, Snowdonia and Anglesey.

The nearby village of Llanaelhaearn has made a name for itself through its enterprise in launching a co-operative initiative which has brought new life to the community.

LLYN ALAW
GWYNEDD B2

This 3-mile-long man-made reservoir, surrounded by rolling, fertile farmlands in the northern part of the Isle of Anglesey, was created in 1966. At 314 hectares (777 acres), it is by far the largest lake on the island.

The reservoir is a source of much recreational activity. Go first to its small visitor centre at the south-western end of the lake, which contains displays on the area. Llyn Alaw's waters attract many birds, including waders and winter wildfowl. The best birdwatching area is at the north-eastern end of the lake, accessible by road from Llanerchymedd, where a reserve and hide have been established. Llyn Alaw is also a good fishing lake, while walkers can follow lakeside footpaths.

The nearby hamlet of Llanbabo contains a tiny 12th-century church with a carving of St Pabo, a king of the Britons who sought refuge on Anglesey in the 6th century.

Llyn Alaw Visitor Centre. Tel (0407) 730762. F. Displays, ranger service, picnic sites.

LLYN BRENIG
CLWYD E3

Llyn Brenig lies in the hauntingly lovely Mynydd Hiraethog, a remote area of moorland and forest, where colours shift constantly in the changing light. Since the lake's opening in 1976 as a storage reservoir for the river Dee it has become popular with visitors seeking outdoor recreation.

The lake's visitor centre provides a stimulating introduction to the archaeology, history, wildlife, geology and engineering of this large stretch of water and the high, bleak moors that surround it. Stone Age man hunted here 7000 years ago. Traces

of his activity remain in discarded flint tools and remnants of fires. Around 4000 years ago, Bronze Age folk lived here. They buried their dead in one of the largest cairnfields yet discovered.

An archaeological trail on the north-eastern shores of Llyn Brenig leads to the ring cairn at Boncyn Arian, a circle of stones and posts where two burial urns containing cremated human remains have been unearthed. In more recent times, 16th-century farmers drove their sheep and cattle to summer grazing on the uplands, moving from 'shore to moor' with the seasons. Remains of the farmers' hafotai (summer dwellings) can also be seen on the trail.

A nature trail, beginning at Pont-y-Brenig on the western shores of the lake, passes through the habitat of the fox, raven and buzzard. Serious walkers prefer a 10½-mile hike around the lake which takes them through osprey and red grouse country.

Sailing at Llyn Brenig

On sunny days the lake shores are crowded with sunbathing families and hardy swimmers dipping in the cool waters. Windsurfers, clinging to brightly coloured sails, skim across the waters. Expert tuition is available to visitors in the lake's windsurfing and sailing school. In designated fishing areas, fishermen cruise gently along in specially designed boats, confident of a good catch in waters which are generously and regularly restocked.

Llyn Brenig Visitor Centre (located near the dam). Tel (049082) 463. F. Provides a fascinating introduction to the lake and its surroundings.

Nearby
Bod Petrual Visitor Centre, Clocaenog forest (located about 4½ miles south-east of the lake on B5105 Cerrigydrudion–Ruthin road). Enquiries to Forestry Commission District Manager, Clawdd Newydd, Ruthin; tel (08245) 208. Clocaenog forest borders eastern shore of Brenig. Past and present forest story told in pictures and dioramas.

The Menai Suspension Bridge, a masterpiece of 19th-century engineering

LLYN CELYN

GWYNEDD   **D4**

Llyn Celyn, in the mountains above Bala, is a 'new' lake created in relatively recent times to supply water to North-east Wales and Cheshire. It doesn't look like a newcomer: thoughtful landscaping, particularly along its grass-covered dam, has resulted in a reservoir that blends in well with its wild surroundings.

Submerged beneath the waters of the lake lies a chapel. There is a memorial to this lost place of worship along the northern shore not far from the road. The modernistic Capel Celyn Memorial, 'designed to resemble a ship coming in from the waters', is built from some of the stones of the original chapel. The memorial also contains three beautifully carved slate tablets bearing the names, dwellings and dates of those buried beneath the lake. Headstones from the original chapel can be seen in a small garden of remembrance nearby.

The rushing river Tryweryn just below the dam is a challenging white-water canoe slalom course.

LLYN CWELLYN

GWYNEDD   **C3**

The A4085 north of Beddgelert runs alongside the waters of Llyn Cwellyn, an attractive lake deep in the mountains cradled by steep slopes. Its far shore is fringed by a conifer plantation, though at the lake's north-western end this gives way to the plunging rock faces of 698m (2290ft) Mynydd Mawr.

MENAI BRIDGE

GWYNEDD   **C3**

Thomas Telford's Menai Suspension Bridge is a magnificent sight. It spans the waters of the Menai Strait, connecting Anglesey with mainland Wales. This bridge presented the most difficult engineering challenge along Telford's London to Holyhead road, now the A5. The elegant, symmetrical structure is 386m (1265ft) long with a central span of 176m (579ft). Completed in 1825, it was the world's first iron suspension bridge. The best overall view of the bridge, which ingeniously takes advantage of a narrow channel where the waters of the strait curl around a wooded promontory, is from the lay-by along the main road west of Menai Bridge town.

The town, which has grown up in the shadow of its famous bridge, is the home of a butterfly farm and the well-established Tegfryn Art Gallery. A delightful garden has been created on a rocky headland overlooking the strait and its sheltered, wooded shores. Just west of the town centre is Church island, linked by causeway to the shore. The car park at the entrance to the Coed Cyrnol woods is the starting point of a footpath through a mature woodland which leads down to the island, on which stands the plain, rough-stoned little Church of St Tysilio. A plaque above its old wooden door reads 'St Tysilio built this church AD630' (the existing church is 15th century).

There is another most attractive walk along the Belgian Promenade, built during World War 1 by Flemish refugees. It starts at the end of the causeway and follows the shore almost all the way

47

to the base of the Menai Bridge. The close-up view of the bridge from underneath brings home the amazing skills of its early 19th-century builders. How did they manage to construct those massive arches – which taper inwards in a most subtle way on their four faces – from such huge blocks of stone?

The faithful bridge is still open to traffic, though the congestion caused by its narrow portals has been relieved by the construction of a second road link a short distance to the west. This is the Britannia Bridge, which has been converted into a double-decker structure to carry a road above Robert Stephenson's railway bridge of 1850.

Pili Palas (on north-western outskirts of town). Tel (0248) 712474. C. Enchanting 'butterfly palace' with tropical jungle and hundreds of exotic butterflies from all over the world. Reptile house, insectarium, pet's corner, bird house, adventure playground, picnic area.

Tegfryn Art Gallery Tel (0248) 712437. F. Displays by contemporary Welsh artists.

MOELFRE
GWYNEDD   C2

Pebble beach and pretty cottages at Moelfre

This attractive village, midway along the Isle of Anglesey's eastern coast, clusters around a rocky foreshore and pebbly cove. Moelfre's rugged coastline has claimed many ships in winter storms. A path north from the village leads to a monument recalling the wrecking of the *Royal Charter*, which sank offshore only hours from the end of a voyage from Australia to Liverpool in a storm in 1859 with the loss of over 400. Charles Dickens came here to record the story of the shipwreck, many victims of which are buried at the churchyard in nearby Llanallgo. Vigilance is still the order of the day along these jagged shores, a fact emphasized by the presence of a lifeboat station at Moelfre.

A cliff path south leads to Traeth Bychan, a large sandy beach sheltered by headlands and popular with sailing enthusiasts. North-west of Moelfre – and also accessible by coast path – is another superb beach at Traeth Lligwy, an expansive area of firm sands backed by dunes. At its northern extremity, Traeth Lligwy joins Traeth-yr-ora, a quiet sandy beach. Next door is Dulas Bay at the mouth of a

silent, remote backwater, a refuge for wildlife almost cut off from the open sea by a bar of land.

Anglesey is renowned for its prehistoric sites. In the countryside a mile or so west of Moelfre stands a formidable monument to our distant past in the shape of the Lligwy Burial Chamber, which dates from late neolithic (New Stone Age) and early Bronze Age times. This huge tomb is capped by a massive stone 5½m (18ft) long by 4½m (15ft) wide weighing 28 tonnes, one of the largest in Britain. When the tomb was excavated in 1908, the bones of adults, children and animals were uncovered.

In the fields nearby is the Din Lligwy Hut Group, the remains of an ancient village settlement, covering about ¼ hectare (½ acre), dating from the late Roman period in Wales. The stone foundations of the huts can still be seen within the remnants of an enclosure wall. Excavations here have revealed Roman coins and pottery of the 4th century AD. Capel Lligwy, also nearby, is a small roofless chapel, simply built in stone, which dates from the 12th century.

Nearby
Din Lligwy Hut Group (in fields off minor road about ¾ mile north of Llanallgo). F. Remains of ancient village. Capel Lligwy nearby. ✚

Lligwy Burial Chamber (beside minor road about ½ mile north of Llanallgo). F. Giant prehistoric tomb. ✚

MOLD ℹ
CLWYD   F3

Walkers trekking along the Offa's Dyke Path over Moel Fammau, the Clwydian Range's highest peak, often choose to drop down to rest in nearby Mold, a town famous for its promotion of Welsh culture. North Wales's premier arts and entertainment centre is located here at Theatr Clwyd. In addition, a Museum and Day Centre, established in memory of the famous Welsh novelist Daniel Owen, attracts students from all over Wales.

Mold is steeped in history. Bailey Hill is the site of an early Norman castle. The town's richly ornamented parish church was built to commemorate the victory of Welshman Harri Tudur (Henry Tudor) at Bosworth Field in 1485. It is one of the finest ecclesiastical buildings in Wales containing an unrivalled profusion of heraldic decorations.

Bustling open-air markets lure visitors into the town centre on Wednesdays and Saturdays. There is a daily indoor market too but, if cattle trucks and Land Rovers are seen passing through the streets, it is worth following them to the local cattle market to watch the rapid-fire bidding for livestock.

In the Alyn valley 3 miles west of Mold is the beautifully wooded Loggerheads Country Park, a fascinating place to explore in all seasons. Nature trails lead into grassy clearings filled with wild flowers and alive with birdsong. From the limestone outcrops of Loggerhead rocks a rural landscape sweeps up to the bracken-covered slopes of Moel

Fammau in a multi-coloured patchwork of fields, farms, trees and hedges. There was once a huge lead mine in this area. Its waste tips, water channels and wheel pit are still visible amongst the trees. The perfectly restored Pentre Watermill is the corner-stone of interest in Loggerheads. It is unique in that its history and restoration have been lovingly recorded by David Williams, grandson of the miller, whose family owned the mill from mid-19th century.

Daniel Owen Museum and Day Centre. Tel (0352) 4792/1 F. Attached to town library.

Theatr Clwyd. Tel (0352) 55114. Theatres and cinemas.

Nearby
Loggerheads Country Park (3 miles west of Mold on A494). Tel (0352) 85586. F. Lovely natural setting with fascinating evidence of mining. Pentre Watermill (C) located in park.

NANT GWRTHEYRN
GWYNEDD · B4

The 'ghost village' and former quarrying community of Porth-y-nant was an eerie place of abandoned terraced cottages until it received a new lease of life as a centre for Welsh language studies. There's only one way to reach this captivating little village: on foot, down the valley of Nant Gwrtheyrn.

The village sits at the base of quarry-scarred cliffs where the steep valley meets the sea. The old pier survives, a reminder of the fact that most of the village's supplies used to arrive the easy way, by sea. Approach via Llithfaen, park on the top of the cliff and walk down the track through 'Vortigen's Valley'. The Celtic chieftain Vortigen is said to have invited the Saxons to Britain, paying for his calamitous deed by becoming a fugitive and dying in this 'gloomy hollow'.

NANTLLE
GWYNEDD · C3

Debris from a long history of slate mining gives Nantlle a strange beauty. Scooped, scarred hillsides lie next to unspoilt sheep pastures, and terraced cottages share the valley with small farmsteads, the entire scene presided over by high, challenging mountains. Drive eastwards along the B4418, past the lake of Llyn Nantlle-uchaf, and you soon leave evidence of old industrial activity behind as the road climbs through the foothills of Snowdonia.

Richard Wilson Arts Centre. Tel (0286) 880676. Named after the renowned 18th-century Welsh landscape painter who was inspired by the natural beauty of the Nantlle valley. Centre's main purpose is residential courses but there are occasional exhibitions open to the public (F).

Nearby
Inigo Jones Slate Works, Groeslon. Tel (0286) 830242. C. Self-guided tours of a fully operational slate works, established in 1861. Craftsmen at work making a wide range of slate products using skills and machines unchanged for 100 years.

NEFYN
GWYNEDD · B4

Stylish hotels and restaurants have sprung up on the steep streets of Nefyn, which once made its living from the herring industry. The sea brings another catch now: holidaymakers, who come here to enjoy Nefyn's sheltered coastal setting. Two miles of sandy beach link the three resorts of Nefyn, Morfa Nefyn and Porthdinllaen in a pair of horseshoe curves on Llŷn's northern shore. Things might have been so different had this safe anchorage succeeded in its 19th-century plan to become a major Irish Sea port, a role which went instead to Holyhead.

Swimming is safe here, and there are scenic trails leading along the sea-cliffs. Seaside villas and large semi-detached houses have transformed the western side of Nefyn into a typical coastal resort, but the centre of the village still has an intimate feel. Its past way of life is described in a small maritime museum in St Mary's Church, whose tower supports a sailing ship weathervane.

Llŷn Historical and Maritime Museum, St Mary's Church, Church Street. Tel (0758) 720308 C. Nefyn's maritime traditions remembered.

Nefyn offers its visitors an excellent choice of sandy beaches

WHAT TO DO ON A RAINY DAY

Take a tour through the Sygun Copper Mine

Entertainment-packed Starcoast World

Riding through the Llechwedd Slate Caverns

North Wales was one of the first of Britain's holiday areas to admit to – and take steps to compensate for – the fact that it has been known to rain occasionally. Ironically, it was the resort of Rhyl, known as 'Sunny Rhyl' because of its good sunshine record, that took the plunge and pioneered a new all-weather development. The success of its Sun Centre speaks for itself. A guaranteed climate, tropical beach area and imaginatively designed indoor pool ensure that visitors to the resort have no weather worries.

The Deeside Leisure Centre at Queensferry is another indoor attraction that has really made a name for itself – take the children skating on its large ice rink, the only one in North Wales. Pwllheli's Starcoast World is also packed with all-weather attractions, including a pool with exciting water features.

It may be heretical to mention this, but some attractions are glad when the skies turn from blue to grey. The underground chambers at the Llechwedd Slate Caverns, Blaenau Ffestiniog, are always busy on a rainy day – as is the neighbouring Gloddfa Ganol Mountain Centre, based at the largest slate mine in the world.

Llanberis offers visitors yet another spellbinding underground experience. Here, you are taken on a ride into the heart of a mountain through huge tunnels which are part of an awesome scheme designed to generate hydro-electricity. On a smaller, less high-tech scale, you can glimpse into the world of the Victorian miner at the Sygun Copper Mine near Beddgelert.

There's one attraction on the Isle of Anglesey which surrounds its visitors with water without getting them wet, even on a rainy day. At the popular Anglesey Sea Zoo, you can walk through a realistic 'shipwreck' area and watch fish swimming alongside – and even above – you in specially designed tanks. The Caernarfon Air World, housed in a large converted hangar, contains aeroplane and helicopter displays which will fascinate the children. Adults might prefer the luxurious surroundings of National Trust properties such as Anglesey's Plas Newydd, Bangor's Penrhyn Castle or Wrexham's Erddig Hall.

The kitchen, Erddig Hall

Llanddwyn island juts into the waters of Caernarfon Bay

NEWBOROUGH

GWYNEDD B3

Newborough's most un-Welsh name derives from the time when a 'new borough' was established here in 1303, the result of the English king Edward 1 uprooting and relocating the community at Beaumaris in order to build his mighty castle there. For the last few hundred years until the 1920s, the village was mainly involved with the weaving of marram grass into baskets, mats and ropes. The grass grew on Newborough's huge dune system, which extends from the village all the way to the mouth of the Menai Strait.

The village, in the south-western corner of Anglesey, stands in an area quite unlike the remainder of the island. Beyond Newborough lies a strange mixture of land- and seascapes – a flat expanse of dune, sand, saltmarsh and conifer plantation. Planting began in 1947 to stabilize the shifting sands. The woodland now covers some 809 hectares (2000 acres), combining the interests of forestry and nature conservation. Newborough warren, next to the forest, is one of Britain's largest expanses of sand dunes and an important wildlife refuge.

Newborough's forest and warren stretch from the saltmarshes of the Cefni estuary and Malltraeth sands to the southern entrance of the Menai Strait. Much of the area has been declared a National Nature Reserve. Access is by minor road leading south-west from the village, which winds its way through the pine forest to a large car park and information point. These stand next to an enormous sandy beach with wonderful views across to Snowdonia and the mountainous spine of the Llŷn peninsula.

Llanddwyn island, along the beach, is a rocky promontory nearly 1 mile long usually accessible by foot (except during the highest of tides). A tower, built in 1800 to warn off shipping, was supplemented by a lighthouse in 1873. The island was inhabited as early as the 5th century, when St Dwynwen, patron of lovers, settled here. The remains of a church dedicated to her date from the 16th century.

The area appeals to visitors of all kinds. Those looking for wide, open sands can enjoy one of the best beaches in North Wales. Outdoor and wildlife enthusiasts can follow paths through the woods and across the dunes.

Nearby
Anglesey Bird World, Dwyran (on A4080 about 1¹/₂ miles east of Newborough). Tel (024879) 627. C. Over 1000 tropical birds ranging from parrots to ostriches. Also goats, sheep, donkey rides.

Bryntirion Open Farm, Dwyran (off A4080 about 2 miles east of Newborough). Tel (0248) 430232. C. Family attraction at a working farm. Antique machinery, hatchery, milking, rare breeds, organic food, children's play area.

OVERTON

CLWYD F4

The cooing of turtle doves greets visitors entering Overton's peaceful St Mary's churchyard. They roost in a ring of ancient yew trees, listed amongst the traditional 'Seven Wonders' of Wales. These venerable trees appear both to guard the noble red sandstone church, and to enhance the precinct's air of quiet seclusion. The village streets with their muddle of buildings built of half-timbering and

51

mellow pink bricks have a Sunday afternoon air, rather like the timeless feel of an old English village.

Several charming villages lie in this border region. Close by is Erbistock, renowned as one of the most beautiful hamlets on the river Dee and famous for its 13th-century riverside inn. Penley, like Hanmer, is an attractive village though the latter can also boast a lovely water mere. Bangor on Dee, yet another ancient village, grew up around its attractive 17th-century bridge. There is a famous racecourse nearby where steeplechasing and National Hunt racing occurs according to the season.

Nearby
Bangor on Dee Racecourse. Tel (0948) 860438. C. Enjoy a day at the races.

PENMACHNO
GWYNEDD   D3

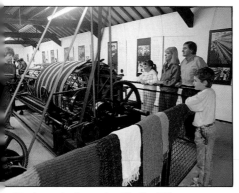

Weaving at the Penmachno Woollen Mill

The most spectacular approach to this village, locked away in the mountains near Betws-y-coed, is from the south along the minor road off the B4407 which snakes across the high, trackless wastes of the Migneint moorlands before dropping abruptly into the valley carved by the river Machno. Penmachno's setting couldn't be more typical. The village shelters in a green valley beneath steep slopes which hill sheep farmers share with conifer plantations.

Penmachno grew up as a quarrying village. Its church contains a noteworthy collection of inscribed early Christian burial stones. In the hills to the northwest is Tŷ Mawr Wybrnant, a little cottage with a cultural significance that belies its modest size. William Morgan was born at this spot in c.1540. Morgan, who later became Bishop Morgan, made a major contribution to the survival of the Welsh language by completing the first full translation of the Bible into Welsh in 1588. The translation has been called 'probably the most important book in the history of the language and literature of Wales'.

Visitors can see weavers at work at the Penmachno Woollen Mill which stands beside the B4406 just north of the village. A little further north-east, near the junction of the B4406 and the A5 and the confluence of two rivers, the Conwy and Machno, is a series of dramatic waterfalls. The Conwy Falls tumble through a wooded gorge, the river then flowing through the Fairy Glen, a famous beauty spot which can be explored by footpath from the falls.

Penmachno Woollen Mill. Tel (0690) 710545. F. Working mill open to the public.

Nearby
Tŷ Mawr Wybrnant (on minor road 2 miles north-west of Penmachno). Tel (06903) 213. C. Simple stone cottage, dating from the 17th century, which has been restored as near as possible to its original appearance. Trail through the Gwydyr forest. 🌿

PENMAENMAWR
GWYNEDD   D2

Penmaenmawr was reborn as a holiday resort when its new promenade was officially opened in the summer of 1990. The area has been carefully designed for the convenience of visitors. Seaside parking and facilities for the disabled give easy access to sun terraces, grassed areas, a children's playground and paddling pool. The view from Penmaenmawr's long shingle-backed sandy beach is beautiful, looking out across Conwy Bay to Anglesey and Puffin island.

The town's proximity to the heart of Snowdonia makes it an ideal touring base. Start by exploring the mountain walks behind the town. Don't miss the trek or drive into the Sychnant pass, a narrow defile, feared in more violent times as the scene of ambushes (its present road was opened in 1772 as part of the new turnpike road from Conwy to Bangor); or the walk, starting from the town's library, which follows ancient trackways to an Iron Age fort, a Druid's circle, Roman road and neolithic (New Stone Age) axe factory, axes from which have been found all over Britain.

PENMON
GWYNEDD   C2

Penmon Priory, near the eastern tip of Anglesey, is a site of great antiquity. It was probably founded as a monastery in the 6th century by St Cynlas and St Seiriol, though as it now stands it dates mainly from the 12th and 13th centuries when Augustinian monks took over. The monks lived in the priory range, the extensive ruins of which reveal a building with a cellar, refectory and dormitory. Next door is a medieval place of worship, still in use as the parish church.

The unusual domed stone structure nearby is a dovecot, built in about 1600 to hold nearly 1000 birds. Penmon is also the site of a holy well of ancient origins. Follow the road north-eastwards for a short distance to the viewpoint overlooking Puffin island, site of another monastic settlement founded by St Seiriol.

Penmon Priory. F. Interesting ruins and holy well in tranquil location. ✠

WELSH WORDS EXPLAINED

Welsh placenames can tell us a lot about the town, village, area or mountain in question. Many Welsh placenames are based on local physical or geographic features, such as rivers, hills, bridges, woodlands and so on. Aber, for example, means 'mouth of', so Abersoch means 'The mouth of the river Soch'.

Here are a few examples of Welsh names you'll come across on your travels:

aber	confluence, rivermouth
afon	river
bach, fach	small
ban, fan	peak, crest
blaen	head, end, source
bryn	hill
bwlch	pass
caer, gaer	fort, stronghold
carreg	stone, rock
castell	castle
cefn	ridge
clawdd	hedge, ditch, dyke
coch, goch	red
craig, graig	rock
crib	crest, summit, ridge
cwm	valley, cirque
cymer	meeting of rivers
dinas	fort, city
du, ddu	black
dyffryn	valley
eglwys	church
ffin	boundary
glyn	glen
gwaun, waen	moor, mountain pasture
hendre	winter dwelling, permanent home
heol	road
llan	church, enclosure
llwyn	grove, bush
llyn	lake
llys	hall, court
maen	stone
mawr, fawr	great, big
merthyr	church, burial place
moel, foel	bare hill
mynydd, fynydd	mountain, moorland
pant	hollow, valley
pen	head, top, end
pentre	village, homestead
plas	hall, mansion
pont, bont	bridge
sarn	causeway, old road
tre, tref	hamlet, home, town
uchaf	upper, higher, highest
ystrad	valley floor

A FEW GREETINGS

bore da	good morning
dydd da	good day
prynhawn da	good afternoon
noswaith dda	good evening
nos da	good night
sut mae?	how are you?
hwyl	cheers
diolch	thanks
diolch yn fawr iawn	thanks very much
croeso	welcome
croeso i Gymru	welcome to Wales
da	good
da iawn	very good
iechyd da!	good health!

PENRHYNDEUDRAETH

GWYNEDD   C4

This unpretentious small town stands on the busy A487 between Maentwrog and Porthmadog. It provides access to the toll road across the mouth of the river Dwyryd, which cuts miles off the journey along the coast to the south. The street leading down to the toll road has a viewpoint over the estuary. There's an unexpected choice of small shops on the Beddgelert road out of town. The entrance to the unique Italianate village of Portmeirion, creation of the architect Sir Clough Williams-Ellis, is on the A487 on the western approach to the town (see Portmeirion entry).

PENSARN

CLWYD   E2

The coastline at Abergele (see separate entry) consists of miles of sand. At Pensarn and Towyn the shores that were devastated in the winter floods of 1989/90 have sprung back to life with confidence in their future. At Pensarn pleasure beach visitors can sample anything from bingo and slot machines to a tummy-twisting roll on a bouncing castle.

In summer, Towyn's flowerbeds are a blaze of colour reflecting the colourful atmosphere of arcades, pubs and eating places decked out in their new liveries. The refurbished fairground swallows up friends old and new amongst amusement machines, waltzers, go-karts, trampolines and 'The Convoy', a new and lively kiddies' ride.

The new American-style Harness Racing track on Towyn Road is presented, in the true USA way, with lots of razzmatazz. Exciting harness races, stage-coach and rodeo competitions, and chariot races all draw enthusiastic crowds.

Nearby
Tir Prince Raceway, Towyn. Tel (0745) 345123. C. American-style harness racing.

PENTREFOELAS

CLWYD **D3**

In its heyday the inhabitants of the manorial village of Pentrefoelas could contribute 37 vocations to the well-being of their community, including:

A labourer, gravedigger, carpenter of skill,
A baker, a barber and the man of the mill.

Now that the heart of the old village has been designated a conservation area, its many decayed stone buildings have been restored to accommodate viable businesses.

Visitors follow a Heritage Trail which leads via shops, a smithy, an iron workshop and a cabinet maker to a working watermill. Inside the mill, time is thrown out of gear as the miller sets massive old grindstones spinning to turn wheat into flour. The mill environment, from its waterwheel and pigsties to its display of obsolete farming implements, is in perfect order.

The village's past speaks aloud in its datestones, single-arch bridges, stone walls, huge chimneys and in the inn whose stables once housed 100 horses to serve the stagecoach service from London to Holyhead.

Pentrefoelas is a village that has refused to die. A visit here will help you understand why this precious example of Welsh country life is being rescued from oblivion by the energy and imagination of its people.

Pentrefoelas Watermill. Tel (06905) 343. C. Working mill producing flour.

PORT DINORWIC

GWYNEDD **C3**

Port Dinowric is an unusual place in the throes of transition. The banks of its wooded creek, over-looked by a marina-style housing development, bristle with the masts of sleek yachts. Close by is the unadorned Port Dinorwic of old, a reminder of its roots as a working port. The tall-walled harbour,

Well-placed Port Dinorwic is a good sailing centre

next to an area of rough ground presided over by a solitary old chimney, would have been the scene of hectic activity in the 19th century when Port Dinorwic was busy shipping slate from the quarries at nearby Llanberis.

The port allows almost instant access to the fine sailing waters of the Menai Strait. A few miles to the south-west is Plas Menai, a superbly equipped and sited watersports centre.

PORTHMADOG

GWYNEDD **C4**

Everything about Porthmadog suggests the seaside: its fresh sea air, its sailing boats and its seagulls. The only thing that seems to be missing is the sea – which is actually around the corner. Porthmadog sits on the Glaslyn estuary, and was originally – and relatively recently – the creation of one ambitious man. William Madocks, a 19th-century MP, decided to reclaim 2800 hectares (7000 acres) of land from the rivermouth in the hope of catching the tourists

The narrow-gauge Ffestiniog Railway travels all the way to Blaenau Ffestiniog

heading for ferries to Ireland. His grand scheme was based on establishing a mail route from London to Ireland via Porthdinllaen on the Llŷn peninsula. It involved building The Cob, a mile-long embankment which nowadays carries traffic across the estuary for a small fee, and also brought nearby Tremadog into being (see separate entry). The plan failed when Holyhead, on Anglesey, became the major ferry departure point, and tourist traffic was diverted away from Llŷn.

It was slate that eventually made Porthmadog's money. The narrow-gauge Ffestiniog Railway, which runs along The Cob, is a reminder of the days when slate was transported 13½ miles from the quarries at Blaenau Ffestiniog to Porthmadog's quayside to be shipped all over the world. The steam trains have resumed their trips through the beautiful Snow-donia landscape, but now carry holidaymakers in place of their original cargo.

Snowdonia meets the sea at Porthmadog harbour

Porthmadog itself is a busy resort whose High Street shops bring in a lively trade throughout the summer. The harbour, overlooked by hills and colourful terraced houses, is part of a popular marina and yachting centre. Among its attractions is a Maritime Museum, where the area's shipping history is traced.

There's a good range of galleries and craft shops in town, including the pottery at the bottom of Heol y Wyddfa (Snowdon Street): just look out for the huge painted mural which tells the Porthmadog story on the outer wall. As well as a shop and work studio, the pottery offers visitors a lesson in pot-throwing (you can keep the end result).

Near the British Rail station, at the opposite end of town, is another narrow-gauge railway, the Welsh Highland, which so far travels only a mile into the countryside and stops at Pen y Mount. At the guard's discretion passengers can visit the sheds at Gelert's Farm Halt, where locomotives and rolling stock are kept.

To complete the seaside effect, there are two beaches within easy reach of Porthmadog: one at nearby Borth-y-gest (sand and pebble), and one at Morfa Bychan, where the dunes of Black Rock sands stretch for 2 miles. Swimming is limited at both, due to strong currents; stay close to the shore at Borth-y-gest, and away from the south-eastern end of Black Rock sands.

Ffestiniog Railway. Tel (0766) 512340/831654. C. One of the most popular of Wales's 'Great Little Trains'.

Madog Motor Museum, Heol y Wyddfa (Snowdon Street). C. Display of vintage motorcycles and cars.

Maritime Museum. Tel (0766) 513730/312804. C. Quayside museum housed in last remaining slate shed.

Porthmadog Pottery, Heol y Wyddfa (Snowdon Street). Tel (0766) 512137. C. Try your hand at throwing your own pot.

Welsh Highland Railway, Gelert's Farm Works, Madoc Street West. Tel (0766) 513402. C. Runs through pleasant countryside.

PORTMEIRION
GWYNEDD   C4

Portmeirion is one of the few places that almost defies description. The visual extravagance of this fantasy village eclipses all attempts to pin it down in words. Italianate, eccentric, strange, charming, bizarre, amusing, disorienting ... these are just some of the impressions which visitors to this unique place come away with. This would have pleased Portmeirion's creator, architect and iconoclast Sir Clough Williams-Ellis, who built the village piecemeal over the years between 1925 and 1972.

Portmeirion, which nestles on a wooded hillside on its own wooded peninsula overlooking a dreamy view of sand, sea and mountain, is much more redolent of southern Italy than North Wales. Sir Clough's village consists of colour-washed buildings, fountains, statues, columns and fake façades that front nothing. Look closer at his various creations and you will discover an amazing combination of different architectural styles and influences – everything from oriental to traditional English – reflecting Sir Clough's 'gay, light-opera sort of approach'.

The location for this magic place is perfect: surrounding the village on three sides are sub-tropical woodlands, criss-crossed by miles of paths leading to beaches of gleaming sand.

Portmeirion's ambiguous personality and other-worldly atmosphere came to the fore, of course, when the village achieved massive exposure as the setting for that cult 1960s television series, *The Prisoner*, starring Patrick McGoohan. *Prisoner* fans still make the pilgrimage to this surreal, self-contained spot to relive scenes from the series' baffling story line.

Portmeirion. Tel (0766) 770228. C. Has the atmosphere of a strange, self-contained world. Located in a beautiful spot.

Surreal Portmeirion, one of the world's strangest villages

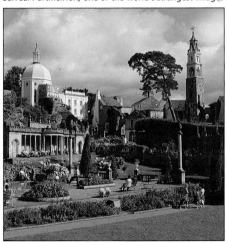

WALKING

In the hills near Capel Curig

There's wonderful walking in the border country around Llangollen

Boulder-strewn Snowdonia

Outdoor enthusiasts have been flocking to North Wales since the early days of travel. Pioneering Victorians scrambled up Snowdonia's rocky screes, attracted to the highest mountains in Britain south of the Scottish Highlands. The appeal of Snowdonia is as powerful as ever – the mountains are nowadays perhaps too popular for their own good, for Snowdon is said to be shrinking a little each year due to erosion caused by the boots of thousands of walkers.

Llanberis is an excellent base from which to explore the Snowdonia National Park's loftiest peaks. From here, a number of footpaths lead to the 1085m (3560ft) summit of Snowdon, though there are also plenty of alternative – and not so well trodden – walking options locally.

North Wales has something for all kinds of walkers. The dedicated enthusiast will inevitably be drawn to Snowdonia's high, wild country. Weekend walkers and family groups will probably prefer easier routes – sometimes waymarked throughout – along riverbanks, beside seashores and through forests.

The mountain resort of Betws-y-coed is at the hub of a network of attractive, gentle walks through the Gwydyr forest, an area of thick woodlands, scenic gorges and rushing rivers. There are also walks around the shores of Llyn Brenig and trails amongst the trees of the nearby Clocaenog forest in the high moorland south of Denbigh.

The springy turf which covers the rounded green hills of the Clwydian Range above the Vale of Clwyd provides a complete contrast to Snowdonia's rocky paths. You'll enjoy exhilarating walking by following sections of the long-distance Offa's Dyke Path which runs along the crest of these hills.

The Offa's Dyke Path also winds its way through the border country around Llangollen. Down in the valley, there's an idyllic towpath walk along the Llangollen Canal, though you'll need a head for heights if you follow the gangway across the Pontcysyllte Aqueduct, which carries the canal 39m (121ft) above the valley.

The walks featured here give just a flavour of the huge variety of trails in North Wales. Local Tourist Information Centres will be happy to supply further suggestions.

An aerial canalside walk across the Pontcysyllte Aqueduct

PRESTATYN

CLWYD   E2

Prestatyn's Nova Centre

Prestatyn's 3 miles of fine sand divide into Barkby, Central and Ffrith beaches. Quiet Barkby Beach is the place to slip your sailing dingy into the sea while the family plays pitch and putt, or picnics on stretches of almost deserted sand.

The indoor Nova complex at Central Beach presents a colourful programme of entertainment day and night: an exciting pool and aquaslide, cabarets, bars, restaurants and discos within a protected all-weather environment. Ffrith Beach boasts the greatest concentration of visitors and attractions. At its hub is the large entertainments centre. A boating lake, crowded with fun and paddle boats, is a top attraction closely rivalled by the go-karts, all-terrain buggies, play area and crazy golf.

Prestatyn's ingredients are those of traditional fun 'beside the seaside' spiced with modern attractions. Children can enjoy good old-fashioned donkey rides and up-to-date amusements. For adults, there's everything from band concerts to discos. Other amenities include a Sports and Recreation Centre in Princes Avenue, a challenging 18-hole golf course and superb indoor bowls facilities at the David Bryant Bowls Centre, Ffrith Beach.

A simple stone pillar next to the Nova Centre above Prestatyn's Central Beach attracts walkers from all over the British Isles. They come to it at the end of a long pilgrimage, following the Offa's Dyke Path which begins 168 miles away in Chepstow, South Wales. Offa, an 8th-century King of Mercia, built the dyke to fix the border between himself and the Welsh. Twelve centuries later Offa's Dyke is the basis of one of Britain's most attractive and rewarding long-distance walks.

The Romans also left their mark on Prestatyn. Tiles with 20th Legion insignia have been discovered and, in 1985, parts of 2000-year-old buildings – including the massive oak stump which had supported a wooden aqueduct – were unearthed in the town. Historical links like these add dignity and style to Prestatyn's status as a popular seaside resort.

Ffrith Beach Entertainments Centre. Tel (0745) 854394. Fun for all ages.

Nova Centre, Central Beach. Tel (0745) 888021. C. Colourful indoor complex.

PWLLHELI

GWYNEDD   B4

Pwllheli's long beaches have been attracting visitors for over 100 years. Its genteel seafront and 5 curving miles of sand and shingle are well designed for a quiet beach holiday, though swimming is not safe near Gimblet rocks or the harbour. A five-minute walk along Ffordd y Cob (Embankment Road) leads past the harbour, the location of a sailing centre and boat club, to a completely different Pwllheli: the old market town, whose narrow streets and crowded shops have retained a quite separate character. An open-air market is held every Wednesday on the Maes (square), an area close to small cafés and arcaded shops.

A wide range of sports and activities is on offer in the new Dwyfor Leisure Centre, including squash,

Loop the loop at Starcoast World, near Pwllheli

keep-fit, a sauna and solarium. North-east of Pwllheli, off the A497, a bumpy single-track road leads to Pennarth Fawr, a 15th-century high-roofed hall which, before the days of chimneys, was heated by a central hearth. A wooden stepladder leads to the upper 'floor', a platform taking up a third of the hall's length. Next door is a pottery where you can pick up a guide to the hall and its history.

Halfway to Criccieth, further east on the A497, Butlin's have created an imaginative huge palace of leisure, known as Starcoast World, which is still expanding. Blood-curdling rides include the 'Boomerang' roller coaster; one of the longest chairlifts in Britain travels to the beach; and there are all kinds of inventive indoor alternatives to the sea, such as a 'sub-tropical' pool complete with rapids and a whirlpool. The centre is open to non-residents by day ticket.

Dwyfor Leisure Centre, Ffordd Caerdydd (Cardiff Road). Tel (0758) 613437. C. Indoor sports for the energetic and relaxation to recharge the batteries.

Nearby
Bodvel Hall Adventure Park (on A497 midway between Pwllheli and Nefyn). Tel (0758) 613386. C. Family attraction with farmyard animals, pets' corner, birds of prey, adventure playgrounds, craft workshop, fishing, putting green.

Pennarth Fawr (on minor road off A497, 3 miles north-east of Pwllheli). F. Interesting medieval house, one of the few of its kind in Wales. ✠

Starcoast World (north-east of Pwllheli on A497). Tel (0758) 612112. C. Leisure complex with exciting rides and excellent all-weather facilities, including superb pool.

QUEENSFERRY
CLWYD   F3

Road bridges over the Dee have long since swept Queensferry's ferry boats into history. Visitors flock to the immense range of facilities offered by the town's Deeside Leisure Centre whose top attraction is its international ice rink. Everyone enjoys watching ice-hockey, curling, ice-galas and displays but young people love to join in the 'Disco on Ice' sessions. At Sandycroft there is an indoor go-karting centre.

Constant building development has linked Queensferry to Connah's Quay where visitors will find Wepre Country Park, once the hunting ground of a large estate and the location of the ruined 13th-century Ewloe Castle (see Hawarden entry). The ancient woodlands are mentioned in the *Domesday Book* of 1086. In the park's visitor centre, itself built on an old Saxon site, displays describe the area's history, flora, fauna and waterways.

Deeside Leisure Centre. Tel (0244) 812311. C. Major sports and leisure complex with ice rink.

Nearby
Wepre Park, Connah's Quay. Tel (0244) 814931. F. Wooded valley with nature trails, visitor centre, events programme, guided walks and ranger service.

RHIW
GWYNEDD   B4

Rhiw is a tiny community close to the south-western tip of the Llŷn peninsula. This is wild, windswept country, with a coastline that has a savage reputation for shipwrecks. The exposed, deserted 4-mile-long bay known as Porth Neigwl or Hell's Mouth (the colourful English description is not a translation of the Welsh) has for centuries commanded the utmost respect amongst sailors, especially when south-westerlies blow directly on to its unprotected shores. This is a beach for those who like the sands all to themselves. Surfing conditions are often excellent, though bathing is not recommended in rough weather.

Plas-yn-Rhiw looks down on to this scene from a sheltered hillside on the western flank of Porth Neigwl. This small manor house, medieval in origin but mainly of the 17th century, stands amongst luxuriant woodlands and ornamental gardens.

Plas-yn-Rhiw. Tel (075888) 219. C. Compact manor house with fascinating history, standing in lush grounds. Its rooms are full of period interest. 🦋

Porth Neigwl's wild coastline has claimed many ships

RHOSNEIGR
GWYNEDD   B3

Rhosneigr is set on a low-lying stretch of Anglesey's western shores. The pleasant little resort has generous stretches of broad sands interspersed with rocky outcrops and separated by a headland. From the beach of Traeth Crigyll there are splendid views northwards along the coast. The sands curve around the headland and continue south to become Rhosneigr's second beach, Traeth Llydan.

The road into the village runs between dunes and the reedy shores of Llyn Maelog. There is an excellent 18-hole golf course nearby. Some of Anglesey's many prehistoric sites are also located close by. The Tŷ Newydd Burial Chamber is accessible by minor road off the A4080 about ³/₄ mile north-east of Llanfaelog. The most famous tomb, though, is Barclodiad y Gawres. Its name, meaning 'The Giantess's Apronful', is expressive of its impressive size. One of the most interesting of Wales's neolithic

(New Stone Age) burial tombs, it contains rare examples of prehistoric art in the form of patterns cut into the stones within its passageway and chambers. The mound of the tomb, which contains a 6m (20ft) passage leading to a central chamber, has been restored to its original condition.

Nearby
Barclodiad y Gawres Burial Chamber (on headland 1¹/₂ miles south-east of Rhosneigr, a short walk from Porth Trecastell beach on A4080). F. Spectacularly sited tomb which contains prehistoric rock carvings. ✤

RHUDDLAN
CLWYD   E2

In earlier times Rhuddlan was considered strategically important because it could be reached by sea-going vessels. Its historic significance rests in Edward I's Statute of Rhuddlan, which in 1284 decreed a code of laws assimilating Wales with England.

The Normans constructed a motte and bailey on Twthill which was superseded in the 1280s by a castle built by Edward I. The king included Rhuddlan in his 'ring of iron' – a chain of castles stretching across North Wales to contain and crush the rebellious Welsh princes. Edward also canalized the river Clwyd to enable the castle to be supplied from the sea. As a result the town prospered as a port until the coming of the railways in the late 19th century.

Though the present town is comparatively new, a walkabout reveals traces of Rhuddlan's long history. Scattered archaeological excavations have exposed Roman pottery and earthworks and the foundations of a Norman church and chapel. The medieval stone bridge dates from 1595 and the farmyard of Plas Newydd holds the remains of a 13th-century Dominican priory. Bodrhyddan Hall lies 1 mile to the east (see Dyserth entry).

Rhuddlan Castle and Twthill. Castle (C) at present undergoing restoration but partially open to the public. Twthill F. ✤

Rhuddlan Castle

RHYL ⓘ
CLWYD   E2

Miles of golden sands where families enjoy traditional British seaside entertainment constitute the foundation of Rhyl's success as one of Wales's premier holiday venues. But sand and sea alone no longer satisfy the modern visitor. Rhyl's response has been a huge financial investment in facilities worthy of the 1990s. Imagine lying stretched out beneath palm trees watching the children romp in a tropical lagoon, in a land where it never rains; that's Rhyl's Sun Centre, an innovative development – one of the first of its kind in Wales – providing an all-weather holiday environment of the highest quality.

Good temperatures are guaranteed at the Sun Centre

The exciting new Knight's Caverns promise a fantastic journey through ancient Wales. Shiver your timbers in the eerie semi-dark as goblins, witches and battling knights leap to life through cunning use of tricks and spine-tingling special effects.

Action families can turn out to compete in the tenpin Superbowl where computerized scoring ensures undivided concentration on the game; or pop next door to Ocean Beach to have their blood pressure raised sky-high by the stomach-churning G-forces of waltzers, helter-skelters and other devilish contraptions. Down to earth again along the West Promenade, you can enjoy the more sedate pastimes of mini-golf or boating.

If you want to get away from the bright lights, then go to the quay opposite the mouth of the river Clwyd. From here some of Rhyl's fishing boats will take you sea fishing to sand-fringed Kinmel Bay, or you can simply let the sea breezes whet your appetites on a restful cruise up the coast. Landlubbers can seek out the peace of the beautiful Botanical Gardens or Rhyl Library where, in a

Rhyl's colourful seafront

museum and arts centre, you will find the resort's heritage imaginatively displayed.

There's entertainment for all in the resort's three theatres, including musicals, hypnotism shows, baby and bathing beauty competitions. Full use is made of the ballroom in Rhyl's immaculately refurbished Town Hall for dances and other evening entertainment. Visitors enjoy the convenience of indoor shopping at the White Rose Centre. Finally, let yourself be whisked to the top of the Skytower, where, in a 73m (240ft) perch as high as an eagle's nest, you'll see the coastal and mountain panoramas of North Wales spread out before you.

Coliseum Theatre, Promenade. Tel (0745) 351126. Variety shows.

Knight's Caverns, Promenade. Tel (0745) 338562. C. Mythology and the supernatural intermingle with the story of Welsh history.

Library Museum and Arts Centre, Church Street. Tel (0745) 353814. F. Library with international and local exhibitions.

Little Theatre, Vale Road. Tel (0745) 342229. Children's shows.

Marine Lake and Watersports Centre. Promenade. Tel (0745) 355454. C. Sail, windsurf, canoe, or drive a pedal boat, all without fear of the sea.

New Pavilion Theatre, Promenade. Tel (0745) 344433. Wide variety of entertainment in 1000-seat theatre.

Ocean Beach Amusement Park, Promenade. Tel (0745) 343246. Traditional seaside funfair; laughter, rides and arcades.

Rhyl Sports Centre, Grange Road. Tel (0745) 343337. C. Fully equipped modern leisure centre.

Skytower, Promenade. C. Rhyl's mini Eiffel Tower. Presents a bird's-eye view of North Wales.

Sun Centre, Promenade. Tel (0745) 344433. C. Top-class indoor entertainment centre. Surf, slide and splash; take chances in the Dragon Flume Pool; glide past in style on an overhead railway; relax in any weather.

Superbowl, Promenade. Tel (0745) 342247. C. Ultra-modern tenpin bowling centre.

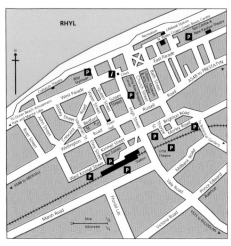

RUTHIN
CLWYD   E3

Ruthin is an architectural gem

This characterful market town stands in the green, fertile bowl of the Vale of Clwyd, sheltered by the Denbigh moors and the Clwydian Range. Ruthin is famous for its well-preserved architecture, a delightful mixture of medieval, Tudor and Georgian influences. Pride of place goes to its 'magpie'-style half-timbered buildings, which dominate the town's central square.

Apart from the cars and a few modern shop frontages, it's like stepping back into the past when you enter St Peter's Square. The bold patterns of black-and-white buildings stand out amongst the more subdued Georgian façades, while the rooflines are an ever-changing jumble of gables and dormers. The Old Courthouse, now a bank, was built in 1401 as the town's court and prison and has been immaculately restored (even the timber pegs which lock the beams together are still in place). A second significant building, the renovated Exmewe House, is again half timbered – and also a bank. The rough block of limestone on the pavement outside is known as Maen Huail (Huail's Stone). According to legend, King Arthur had Huail, his rival in love, beheaded on this stone.

Look out for 'the eyes of Ruthin' – seven Dutch-style dormers – set into the red tile roof of the 17th-century Myddleton Arms. Stagecoaches used to stop at the Castle Hotel next door, a handsome Georgian building. St Peter's Church, at the edge of the square, is full of interest. The church's elegant 55m (180ft) spire, a landmark for many miles around, is the focus for a fascinating collection of buildings that are not only of religious interest. Clustered around the church are old almshouses and the first site of Ruthin's historic grammar school, an institution of medieval origins.

The church was founded in 1310 as a collegiate church. Its old cloisters survive, though St Peter's most outstanding feature is its amazing Tudor roof consisting of hundreds of carved oak squares

There is so much to see in Ruthin – the old gaol, the remnants of a medieval castle (now the site of a hotel and venue for medieval banquets), and more historic buildings such as Nantclwyd House (currently under restoration for eventual opening to the public). Ruthin has the air of an ancient town whose character has not been ravaged by modern development – an impression reinforced by the tradition of ringing the curfew bell at 8pm every night from the churchyard (Ruthin in now the only town in Britain where this still happens) and the 'Medieval Wednesdays' held here in the summer season when townsfolk dress in period costumes.

For a wonderful view of the town in its patch-work valley drive into the Clwydian Range along the minor mountain road which climbs north-eastwards from nearby Llanbedr Dyffryn Clwyd. If you're feeling energetic, you can follow footpaths to Moel Fammau, at 555m (1821ft) the highest point in the Clwydian Range, and marvel not only at the view but at the toil and tenacity of those who built the vast Egyptian-style obelisk here in 1810 to commemorate George 111's Golden Jubilee.

Ruthin Castle Medieval Banquets. Tel (08242) 2664. C. An entertaining evening out.

Ruthin Craft Centre. Tel (08242) 4774/5675. F. Attractive complex of independent studio workshops surrounding a pretty courtyard. A wide variety of crafts on view.

ST ASAPH
CLWYD   E2

The minuscule city of St Asaph holds a special place in the affections of North Walians. It is the proud possessor of the smallest cathedral in Britain, which has twice been destroyed since its foundation in AD537. Its most famous cleric was Bishop William Morgan who, in 1588 with other Welsh bishops, finished translating the Bible into Welsh. A column in the cathedral grounds records their achievement.

The cathedral museum contains stone and bronze implements, Roman coins and the famous Welsh/Greek/Hebrew dictionary compiled by the eccentric 'Dic Aberdaron' (1780–1843). Dic was a strange genius, welcomed in the company of learned men, who reputedly taught himself 35 languages. His gravestone is in the churchyard of the parish church. The church itself is built in traditional Welsh style. Other places of interest in St Asaph include 17th-century almshouses and a five-arched stone bridge over the river Elwy

St Asaph hosts the prestigious North Wales Music Festival for a week each year in late September.

St Asaph Cathedral. Britain's smallest medieval cathedral.

TREARDDUR BAY
GWYNEDD   B2

This resort is on an island which itself is part of a larger island. Trearddur Bay is on Holy Island off the Isle of Anglesey's west coast, though both are connected by road and rail. Trearddur Bay is in a most attractive setting. Its sheltered, sandy bay takes a deep bite out of a rocky, indented shoreline, and there are pleasant walks along the low cliffs in each direction. Golf, sailing and fishing are also popular pastimes at this charming little resort. It is well worth exploring this coastline fully, for you will discover other delightful little bays – such as Porth Dafarch – to the north and south.

A little further south you'll come across more fine coastal scenery around peaceful Rhoscolyn. The main beach here, of firm, south-facing sands, is tucked well away from the open seas between two headlands.

Beautiful sands at Trearddur Bay

TREFOR
GWYNEDD   **B4**

Visitors to this substantial Llŷn peninsula village of stone cottages do not have to look too far to discover its origins. The granite quarries hewn into the slopes high above the rooftops once provided plenty of work for the villagers. There are more reminders of Trefor's granite-producing past along the now-silent quay and pier, though the abiding memory visitors leave with is the stunning view along the coast as the heights of the Yr Eifl mountains plummet dramatically into the sea in a curtain of sheer cliffs.

Cwm Pottery. Tel (028686) 545. F. Wide range of stoneware. Wonderful setting.

TREFRIW
GWYNEDD   **D3**

The Romans first discovered Trefriw's mineral-rich waters. They tunnelled into the mountain to find the liquid bubbling from a fissure in the ground. Later the Victorians were so successful in exploiting its medicinal properties that steamboats, laden with passengers anxious to take the waters in the spa's pump room, used to arrive regularly from Conwy. Today's visitors to the spa can see the original Roman cave and impressive 18th-century stone bath house with its slate bath, and learn all about the spa's long history.

Inside the Trefriw Woollen Mill visitors are provided with ear protectors to dull the din of weaving machines. In underground channels the waters of the river Crafnant drive turbines which provide electric power for the mill. The mill has been

in production for over 150 years. All of the traditional processes in the manufacture of tapestries and tweeds are still carried out on the premises.

In the mountains above Trefriw three lakes – Llyn Crafnant, Llyn Geirionydd and Llyn Cowlyd – attract large numbers of walkers eager to escape into Snowdonia's wild landscapes.

Trefriw Woollen Mills. Tel (0492) 640462. F. A traditional woollen mill in action.

Nearby
Trefriw Wells Spa (1½ miles north of Trefriw on B5106). Tel (0492) 640057. C. Medicinal waters first discovered by the Romans.

TREMADOG
GWYNEDD   **C4**

Most North Wales communities have grown piecemeal over the years. Tremadog is different. It is an early example of well-thought-out town planning, and it shows it. An open square lends a rare sense of spaciousness to the place, an effect complemented by the harmoniously designed range of dwelling around the open area.

For all its stylishness, the town – historically speaking – was a failure. It was developed by entrepreneur and MP William Madocks (see Porthmadog entry) in the 19th century as a staging-post, part of his ill-fated grand plan to establish a new mail and passenger route to Ireland via Porthdinllaen on the Llŷn peninsula (Tremadog's 'London' and 'Dublin' street names are a real giveaway).

T E Lawrence, better known as Lawrence of Arabia, was born here in 1888.

Nearby
Brynkir Woollen Mill, Golan. Tel (076675) 236. F. Long-established woollen mill, where the public can view the entire manufacturing process from raw wool to finished cloth.

TUDWEILIOG
GWYNEDD   **B4**

Tudweiliog's dark-stoned houses sit high on the cliffs looking out from western Llŷn over the Irish Sea. A minor road leads off the B4417 to the coast road, past Rhos-y-llan, whose single-storey buildings and high hedges are designed to withstand strong sea winds. From this road you can reach the sands of Porth Ysgadan, a small, pleasant cove, where currents are strongest near the headlands (which should be avoided by swimmers).

Further to the south-west, the mile-long sandy Traeth Penllech (Penllech Beach) has safe swimming – though again the headland waters can be dangerous. To the north-east of Traeth Penllech is Porth Ychen, a small shingle beach, and to the south-west is Porth Colman, a popular family beach with safe bathing, reached from Llangwnnadl.

SCENIC DRIVES

Llanberis pass

Moorlands above Penmachno

Where to begin? The Llanberis pass, probably the best-known mountain road in North Wales, is a good starting point. But, spectacular though it is, it does sometimes suffer from a little too much traffic on busy summer days, when parking to admire the views can become severely restricted. There are less confined alternatives. Snowdonia also reveals itself in its full glory along Nant Gwynant, which climbs up past two lovely lakes from Beddgelert, and Nant Ffrancon, which cuts through some of North Wales's most dramatic mountain terrain before dropping down to Bangor.

Horseshoe pass

Off-the-beaten-track addicts will find plenty of intriguing minor roads to explore. Take the B4407 across the empty moorlands east of Ffestiniog, then follow the narrow mountain road which dives into the Machno valley and Penmachno. The lakes hidden in the forests above Llanrwst can be reached by a maze of country roads, while the huge area of moorland and forest between Betws-y-coed and Ruthin is crossed by exhilarating routes such as the A543 and B5105.

From the summit of the famous Horseshoe pass above Llangollen you'll enjoy views far and wide – but don't ignore the equally appealing minor roads north of the town which wind their way deep into the hills. Along the North Wales coast, there's an interesting alternative route between Conwy and Penmaenmawr along the Sychnant pass, a turnpike route originally built for coach travellers.

... AND RAIL RIDES

If you want to sit back and concentrate on the scenery, then hop on a train. The northern section of the scenic Cambrian Coast railway runs alongside Tremadog Bay to Pwllheli. British Rail also guarantees a good view to passengers who travel along its service from Llandudno Junction, through the lovely Vale of Conwy and the Snowdonia uplands, to Blaenau Ffestiniog.

The scenery's also superb along North Wales's delightful narrow-gauge lines – the Ffestiniog and Welsh Highland Railways (see Porthmadog entry), the Snowdonia Mountain and Llanberis Lake Railways (see Llanberis entry) and the Bala Lake Railway (see Llanuwchllyn entry).

Enjoy the views from the Bala Lake Railway

63

In recent years, like a phoenix rising from the ashes, Wrexham's old image has been transformed. By successfully revitalizing its commercial base and skilfully exploiting its rich industrial heritage, Wrexham has become a business and tourist centre for the Welsh borderlands.

The town's 15th-century Church of St Giles has a fascinating history. In one incident during the Civil War Parliamentary forces entered the church to steal organ pipes to melt down for bullets. In the churchyard lies the tomb of Elihu Yale (1648–1721), the son of a local family, whose benevolence resulted in the founding of the great American university which bears his name. On his tomb is carved a long epitaph which begins 'Born in America, in Europe bred'. 'Wrexham Steeple', which makes an appearance as one of the traditional 'Seven Wonders of Wales', is a reference to St Giles's richly decorated 41m (136ft) tower, completed in 1520.

Erddig Hall gives visitors an authentic glimpse into bygone life on a country estate

The town's former industrial importance is encapsulated in the Heritage Centre, King Street. Museum-style exhibits explain the town's brewing, steelmaking, coalmining, and bricklaying history.

Wrexham's appeal to visitors has also been enhanced by developments at the Clywedog Valley Heritage Park. In the venerable King's Mill, south-east of the town centre, is housed the Heritage Park Visitor Centre where a tableau illustrates the miller's life and times. On the first floor audio-visual displays tell visitors about other parts of the park: the restored Nant Mill a few miles to the west which focuses on the park's flora and fauna; the Felin Puleston Visitor Centre, which has agricultural displays; and the park's ancient Plas Power wood-land west of Bersham which can be explored by following nature trails. Bersham Industrial Heritage Centre lies at the heart of the valley. Here, 18th-century buildings, once used by 'Iron Mad' John Wilkinson to cast cannon used in the American War of Independence, are being restored.

Historic Erddig Hall on the outskirts of Wrexham has gained a unique reputation as 'the most evocative upstairs-downstairs house in Britain'. Because the Yorke family, owners of the house since 1733, never felt the urge to move with the times, Erddig remained virtually unchanged for generations. Now people flock from all over the world to view, below stairs, its perfectly preserved kitchens, laundries, pantries and servants hall; and upstairs, the sumptuous furnishings of the library, state bedroom and other treasures. Erddig's grounds, stables and workshops, formal garden and country park offer a day's visit in themselves.

Wrexham's plentiful recreational facilities include three swimming pools, a sports and athletics centre, the most modern indoor tennis complex in Britain and, in nearby Acrefair, a leisure centre equipped with wave machines and a tropical pool.

Clywedog Valley Heritage Park. Attractions include: Bersham Industrial Heritage Centre, Bersham. Tel (0978) 261529 F. Free tours based on Clywedog Heritage Park Trail start here.
Felin Puleston Visitor Centre. F. Farm-based displays.
King's Mill Visitor Centre. Tel (0978) 290444. C. Find out all about the Clywedog valley here.

Erddig Hall (on southern outskirts of Wrexham). Tel (0978) 355314. C. A country house with a difference. Described by the last squire as 'the best place in the world'. 🦋

Wrexham Maelor Heritage Centre. 47–9 King Street. Tel (0978) 290048/358916. F.

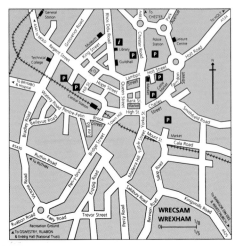